introduction

Manchester? Where the hell is that? The battle for the capital of the north is becoming a one town race. Leeds is the fastest growing city in Europe and that's well reflected in the city's bars, restaurants, clubs and shops. Stand still for long enough and someone's likely to turn you into a café bar. The ultimate guide is back; updated, refreshed and ready to help direct you towards a little hedonism. From the grottiest mosh-pits to the haughtiest of haute-cuisine, you have no excuse not to enjoy yourself.

© itchy Ltd
Globe Quay
Globe Road
Leeds
LS11 5QG
t: 0113 246 0440 f: 0113 246 0550
e: all@itchymedia.co.uk
www.itchycity.co.uk

ISBN 0-9534887-4-8

City Team: John Emmerson, Sally Fairclough Editorial Team: Simon Gray, Ruby Quince, Mike Waugh, Andrew Wood Design: Matt Wood, Tony Ward, Steve Wiseman Cover Design: artscience.net Maps: Steve Cox at Crumb Eye Design
Contributors: Phillipa Black, Jo Grady, Nobby
Jamie Oliver pictures copyright David Loftus

GOJobsite

THIS BOOK HAS THE BEST PLACES TO SPEND YOUR MONEY.

WE HAVE THE BEST PLACES TO MAKE MORE MONEY.

We have hundreds of thousands of new jobs every month from Europe's leading companies. You could find your dream job in seconds, and you might soon need an Itchy Guide to New York, Paris, Sydney…

www.gojobsite.co.uk

contents

- **6** Restaurants
- **28** Bars
- **48** Pubs
- **58** Clubs
- **70** Gay
- **72** Shopping
- **88** Cafés
- **92** Entertainment
- **100** Body
- **106** Takeaway
- **112** Getting About & Accommodation
- **116** Map & Index

foreword

Jamie Oliver

These itchy guides are fantastic. When it comes to travelling, be it social or business, there's so little time to decide where to go and what to do. I spend half my life darting around all over the place, so when I'm visiting cities that I've never been to before, I like to cut to the chase and get to the right places. The itchy guides are just what I've been looking for.

These guides will definitely help you get the most out of a trip to a new city, and whether it's a two hour visit, a night on the town or a long weekend, the itchy team will push you in the right direction. From where you can find the most cutting-edge R'n'B to the coolest threads, as well as some good grub, a few drinks and maybe have a bit of a boogie. And at long last, someone's cottoned on to the fact that once in a while a dodgy pub and a bit of karaoke, beats posing at the latest bar opening, hands down.

It's reassuring to know that the itchy team take their research seriously. I know from experience that they certainly know how to mix business with pleasure.

– Jamie Oliver

---

itchycity.co.uk

For what's happening right here, right now and in 17 other cities... www.itchycity.co.uk. All the events, all the time, with news on gigs, cinema, restaurants, clubs and more. You can sign up for updates on anything from hip hop to happy hours, vent your anger about our reviews and get discounts for your favourite venues. Whatever's happening in the city, itchycity's there.

And for when you're out, we've made that hulking great big wap-phone actually useful. Next time it's 1am and you're gasping for a Guinness, whip out the wap and find your nearest late bar... **wap.itchycity.co.uk**

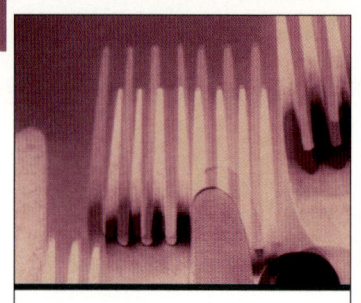

restaurants

www.itchycity.co.uk

With more restaurants than you can shake a chopstick at, half the problem of eating in Leeds is choosing where to go. Let itchy guide you through the minefield of culinary delights on offer in this fair city with our comprehensive guide to the best cooking in the north.

English

Ferret Hall Bistro
North Road, Headingley   275 8613
Not the most obvious choice as it's a way out from town but you'll be pleasantly surprised if you do choose to venture into studentville. This very un-studenty, very small restaurant is patronised, in the main, by the last stronghold of Headingley professionals who doggedly resist the student take-over of the area. The menu is made up of both simple traditional and inspired concoctions – definitely worth battling through the hordes of scholar to sample. There is an early door menu offering a starter and main for £13.95. If you're on a diet they have thoughtfully marked which dishes are low fat.
Mon-Sun: 6-10pm (until 10.30 Fri/Sat).

Cumin marinated pork fillet with pineapple and coconut risotto £10.50, HW £9.95

Calls Grill
The Calls 245 3870

A definite contender for best restaurant in Leeds has deftly taken advantage of the regeneration of this once run-down end of Leeds city centre. Situated in the now upmarket area of The Calls at the back of 'The Exchange Quarter', it tends to attract a more discerning clientele who know their food, although this doesn't mean those on a budget are discriminated against, as the prices are reasonable. Wooden floors blend with earthy brick walls to conjure the feeling of warmth and comfort. If you're lucky you'll be seated at a table overlooking the river, making your visit all the more pleasurable. As for the food, Calls Grill offers a range of mouth-watering options for carnivores and vegetarians alike – you won't find a cheese option simply tacked onto the end of the menu here. It is also worth noting that a new bar is currently under development, providing an ideal place to have pre-drinks before eating whilst also citing The Calls Grill as a quiet drinking venue.

Mon-Sat: 12-2.30/6-10.30pm.
Sun: 6-10.30pm.
Char grilled loin of tuna with a confit of tomatoes and roasted balsamic potatoes £10.95 HW 9.95

THE CALLS GRILL
LEEDS

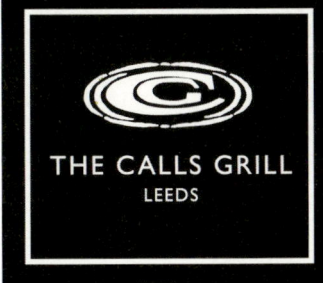

OPEN
MON 6 -10.30
TUE - SAT 12 - 2.30
SUN 6 10.30

38 THE CALLS, LEEDS LS2 7EW
TELEPHONE: 0113 245 3870

Galaxy 105 **THE NEW MIX FOR YORKSHIRE**

restaurants

Harry Ramsdens
White Cross, Guiseley   01943 874 641
The place to reminisce about a face full of fish and chips smothered in tomato ketchup. Without doubt the most famous chippy in the world. The original shed where Mr Ramsden began his little empire is still standing but fortunately the restaurant is a little bigger and more comfortable. The only choice that you really have to make is whether you go for cod or haddock, and if all you really want is a quality takeaway to eat on the Moors nearby, they still have an original chip shop at the side of the building.
11.30-10pm seven days.
Haddock and chips £5.25 HW £7.95
Cup of cha £1.15

Leodis
Sovereign St 242 1010
Exclusive eatery that's full to the rafters of the suited boys from the nearby law firms during the day, and with people either desperate to impress or true foodies in the evening. It's the sort of place you'd expect to find Michael Winner enthusing about and they even have the fat cigars to keep him happy. The only negative is that it can get a little too stuffy; expect derogatory glances if you're not expensively suited and booted.
Mon-Fri: 12-2pm/6-10pm Fri/Sat: 6-11pm.
Veal fried in parmesan crumb, pasta and basil £11.90, HW £11.95

Harvey Nichols 4th Floor
Briggate 204 8000
If you're still reeling from mind-bendingly expensive price-tags downstairs, you can regain composure in this airy restaurant. Prices aren't much better, but you can forget your financial woes with some elegantly prepared cocktails in the stylish bar area. The menu is as you'd expect in such an establishment - sophisticated and unusual, but by and large, you get what you pay for. You could also opt to sit downstairs in the HN Express Bar in the Arcade (and pay a little less).
Open Mon-Wed; 10-6pm, Thurs/Fri: 10-10.30pm, Sat: 9-10.30pm.
Roast Turbot fillet, haricot bean dressing and buttered samphire £14.50.
House wine £11.95

Galaxy 105   THE NEW MIX FOR YORKSHIRE

Pool Court at 42
42 The Calls 244 4242

Location, location, location - the three most important words in the restaurant game. Add to that a Michelin star and food to die for and you've got yourself a contender for the best restaurant in Leeds. The clientele tends to be quite upmarket, but you'd expect nothing less for the prices - a little on the expensive side but this keeps the riff raff out (sob). Dining on the balcony is a must during the day, although it's reserved for drinking during the evening.

Mon-Sat: 12-2pm/7-10pm (until 10.30 Fri/Sat).
Set lunch £19.00 for two courses including Poached supreme of cornfed chicken, House wine 12.95

Shear's Yard
The Calls 244 4144

First thing that hits you is the atmosphere, then the mouth-watering smells. Always bustling with energy, this is a cracking restaurant that's relaxed with a menu to match. Choose from the tapas at the bar, or more substantial mains in the restaurant proper. Usually full of the moneyed crowd from the local flats, it's a salubrious, fairly pricey restaurant. Thursdays see a touch of light jazz, making it a bit like that bar from Ally McBeal. Except quieter. And without Ally.

Open Mon-Sat; 12-2.30pm, 6-10pm (until 10.30pm Thurs-Sat)
Roast guinea fowl, celeriac puree with lime and redcurrant sauce £11.95, HW £9.95

Strawberry Fields
Woodhouse Lane 243 1515

Vegetarians amongst you who have difficulty finding a diverse menu could do worse than check out this popular student restaurant just between both campuses. Situated opposite the BBC, it's popular with the luvvies too (not that Leeds can boast that many, unless you count the Emmerdale C-list celebs). Fairly mixed menu, with cheap offers and an intimate bar upstairs (ie match-box sized).

6pm-10pm throughout the week.
Fajitas £7.99 HW £7.99

Teatro
The Quays 243 6699

A bit off the beaten track, Teatro nestles just to the side of Malmaison on Leeds quay-side. Owned by ex-Leeds United player Lee Chapman and his badly-behaved wife, actress Leslie Ash, Teatro is the ultimate in stylish dining. The open layout is very 'canteen' like, which isn't to my liking, but the food is of a high quality. The service is excellent, it's just that you can't help feeling a bit sorry for the waiting staff who have to satisfy your every whim. Make sure you've got a fat wallet before you leave the house or you'll be left washing the dishes. The place is also home to an exclusive members bar.

Mon-Sat: 12-3pm/6-11.30pm, Sun: 11-4pm.
Grilled tranche of wild halibut with horseradish butter, watercress and new potatoes £14.95 HW £13.00

American

Boston Exchange
St Anne's Lane, Headingley
275 5404
Perfect for those intimate moments when you want to dump your partner. It's quiet most of the time so that no one can hear your feeble-sounding excuses ("I just need some space"). The place is adorned with American tat to talk about in awkward moments ("Don't cry. Hey, that's an interesting number plate."). And the bar's quite cheap with several promotional offers ("It'll be OK. Have a pitcher of Long Island Iced Tea."). Truly soulless.
Mon-Sat: 12-11pm (until 10.30pm Sun).
Enchiladas £8.25

Frankie and Benny's
Cardigan Fields Leisure Park, Kirkstall
203 8888
Who the hell are Franky and Benny? This couple of jokers have set up shop across the UK, with their depressingly formulaic range of burger bars with a 'twist' - they do pasta too! You're just a crazy cat Frankie. And who's idea was it to pipe 50's crooners and Mowtown at disco volume to draw in punters? I bet it was Benny, the cheeky little monkey. The highlight of my visit was the teach yourself Italian audio-cassette being played in the toilets, though it didn't teach me how to say "Can I move my seat to another restaurant?".
11am-11pm seven days.
Fettuccini with smoked salmon £7.25, House wine £7.45

Spirit of St Louis
Boar Lane 245 2555
I've been to St Louis and I think the city should sue for this blatant slur on its character. St Louis is quite a cool place with atmosphere and decent food; this place has neither, in fact it should be called Spirit of St Louis's sewer. It's shit. Wins the esteemed itchy award: The Worst Restaurant in the City.

Congratulations.
Mon-Sat: 11-11pm, Sun: 12-10.30pm.
Cheeseburger with fries £6.25
House wine £7.50

Quincey's
Cardigan Fields Leisure Park, Kirkstall 203 8458
Run of the mill, built-in-a-day restaurant, the only difference being a strongly fish-orientated menu. The prices are higher than its counterparts, but the quality of the food does not warrant the extra cash. If you have an hour before your film at the complex opposite you could stop off for a meal if you're feeling flush, though you'll have to put up with high-five slapping whooping waiters. They actively encourage you to doodle on your paper tablecloths, or you could always eat the crayons if your food's not up to scratch.
Mon-Sat: 12-11pm (until 10.30pm Sun).
Barbecue salmon and scallion mash £9.55, HW £8.90

TGI Fridays
Wellington Street 242 8103
You know the drill - sit down, order and wait for your food. Last time I was here the wait was a little too long and the result was luke warm food. Others swear by this chain with its imported party atmosphere and brace and hat wearing waiting staff. If cocktails are your thing check out the dizzying array of drinks on offers as you sit by the Cheers-type bar. One of the real benefits of TGI is the size of the dishes – go to gorge.
Mon-Sat: 12-11.30pm (until 10.30pm Sun).
Spicy Thai Chicken Noodles £9.75, HW £10.00

French

Café Rouge
Assembly Street 245 1551

Café Rouge is Café Rouge whether you're in Leeds or Leamington Spa. It's red, got French looking waiters, colonial style interiors, a Parisian café atmosphere but sells Franglais food. Good value for money, nice wine, a Saturday shoppers' lunch haven – pleasant. If in doubt give it a go.
Mon-Sat: 10-11pm (until 10.30pm Sun).
Meal for two: £28, Moules.

La Grillade
Wellington Street 245 8856
A cool, cavernous restaurant with a distinctly underground feel. This place attracts a business orientated clientele who enjoy fine food and wine from the company's own vineyard – how posh?

Galaxy 105 THE NEW MIX FOR YORKSHIRE

The staff can be a bit rude, especially if you stumble on the pronunciation of some dishes, but then, they are French.
Mon-Sat: 7-10.30pm.
Cote d'oeuf (for two) £23.50,
House wine £11.50.

Petit Provence
The Headrow 230 7032
There is a streak of genuine authenticity here – simple, but with very good dishes. Perfectly situated for attracting the theatre set as well as those in the know, who prefer not to spend a fortune eating out. The atmosphere is lifting and the décor allows you to enjoy your meal without overbearing fixtures. They have great set-course meal deals but they won't appreciate it if you ask to 'go large'.
Mon-Sat: 7-10.30pm.
Lamb and herb cutlets £8.50 HW £9.50

Rascasse
Canal Wharf, Water Lane
244 6611
On the opposite side of the canal to the majority of Leeds' finer eateries but Rascasse is more than worth the walk. The menu is relatively restricted but inspirationally selected, and although there is limited vegetarian choice the staff are more than willing to concoct a meatless menagerie that would suit even the fussiest veggie. The wine list is more like a James Bond novel than a list, both for it's length and the fact that it visits all four corners of the globe; there's even a few bottles of English.
Mon-Sat: 12-2pm/6.30-9.30pm.
Pre-booked party menu: Roast Onion stuffed with beaufort cheese, tomato risotto, roast fennel and tarragon butter £27.50 (including first course, pudding and coffee too). HW £13.00

Sous Le Nez En Ville
Quebec Street 244 0108
Probably the most extensive fish menu in Leeds, as well as fine English and French fare. Situated behind Majestyks, this underground old timer has been doing well from its reputation as one of the finer restaurants in the city. The prices reflect its prestige, and fortunately the staff are not the usual type employed by expensive restaurants; they're actually courteous with a personality as well. The deep fried brie is one of the most delicious morsels you'll ever sample.

Mon-Sat: 12-2.30pm, Mon-Thurs: 6-10pm, Fri-Sat: 6-11pm.
Pan fried calves liver, red onion and beetroot £10.50, HW £9.50

Italian

Al Bacio
15 Eastgate 245 6566
Traditional pizzeria serving any combination of toppings you can think of. £5.50 deal if you buy any pizza, pasta or dish of the day plus a drink.
**Mon-Sat: 12-2.30pm, evenings 6-11pm. Sunday: 6-11pm.
Diavola (roast chicken in red wine sauce garnished with ham, mushrooms and onions) £6.90, HW £7.90**

Ask
Greek Street 244 1199
Another restaurant jostling for trade on Greek Street is Ask, and if they're finding the competition a bit tough they should try harder. It's good to look at, minimal, airy, light but as we all know, as much as décor is considered important, the quality of the food usually takes priority. It's not bad, it's not great, it's just average. And let it be known, the service here is truly crap. Getting their attention requires lots of shouting and begging, but flicking a dollop of mayonnaise usually does the trick.
**Mon-Sat: 12-12 (until 11pm Sunday).
Napoletana Pizza £5.10, HW £9.50.**

Bibi's
Greek Street 243 0905
A favourite with the suits who populate the silly amount of bars in this area, Bibi's offers a regular Italian meal in somewhat loud surroundings - both the garishly bright interior and the fact it's often hard to hear what your fellow diners are saying. Definitely a place to take the mother-in-law. The prices are slightly more expensive than your average Italian, but if

restaurants   13

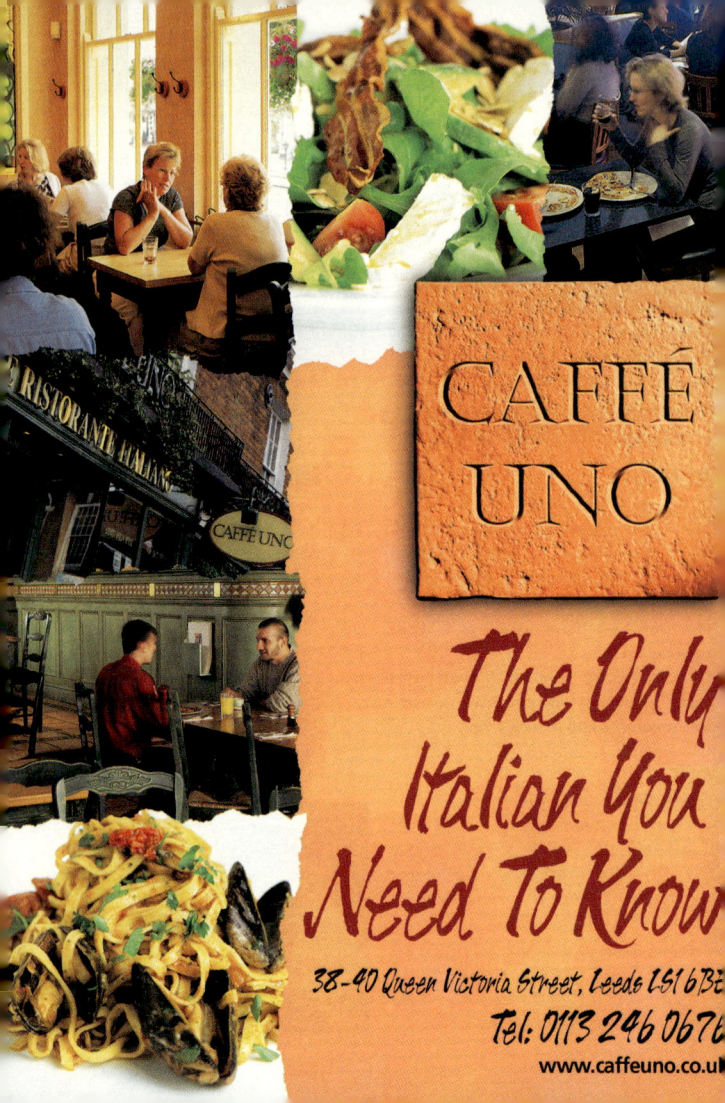

CAFFÉ UNO

The Only Italian You Need To Know

38-40 Queen Victoria Street, Leeds LS1 6BE
Tel: 0113 246 0676
www.caffeuno.co.uk

you enjoy eating in a loud, fast-paced environment you could do worse than try Bibi's.
Mon-Sun: 12-2.15pm/6-11.15pm.
Contadino salad with warm crispy bacon, mustard and chicken £9.00 HW £12.50 per bottle.

Bistro Fiori
8 Commercial St   243 8280
At the centre of the city (opposite WH Smiths) is this quaint and consistently on-form little Italian. Choose from regular Italian delights or something a little different.
Mon-Sat: 12pm-11pm.
Fresh swordfish and watercress with olive oil, lemon and balsamic vinegar £8.50, HW £9.50.

Caffé Uno
Queen Victoria Street, Victoria Quarter 246 0676
With its heated seating area outside you can sit and watch the beautiful people of the Victoria Quarter go by, or chill out in the light-filled room upstairs. It's one of those places with a real community, but with everyone clutching Harvey Nichols bags. Cracking combination of decent Italian nosh, friendly staff and fantastic atmosphere.
Tues-Sat, 8.30am-10.30pm. Mon-Sun, 12pm-10.30pm.
Pollo al masala £9.25.

Da Mario's
The Headrow   246 0390
The best, and biggest, deep fried mozzarella I've ever seen - don't order as a starter if you've got a small appetite. This place is as popular in the day as it is in the evening when shoppers give way to those making their first stop before the theatre, bar or club. Good range of food on offer at reasonable prices, but they do seem to have their off days – on my last visit, both mine and my partner's dish would have failed a Netto's quality test. We complained, they shrugged their shoulders. How very Italian.
Open 12-10.30pm seven days.
Farfalle Puglia (Pasta with tuna, broccoli, garlic and tomatoes) £5.45 HW £7.95 per bottle

Dolce Vita
130 Vicar Lane   242 0565
You know in gangster films when the police arrive someone flicks a switch and turns the illicit gambling den into an impromptu restaurant? Well, this is that restaurant, complete with school tables, paper tablecloths and waiters who quite

Galaxy 105 THE NEW MIX FOR YORKSHIRE

clearly haven't done this before. The food's not bad in all fairness, but eating anything other than pasta turns into a finger-bleeding, hand-aching chore with their shockingly blunt cutlery.
Carbonarra £5.95, HW £9.45

Dino's
Bishopsgate (Under the station car park) 234 4241
A traditional Italian with a big heart located in the centre of Leeds. Don't ask the head waiter to recommend anything – apparently he never eats here (his wife's cooking is too good), so let me do it instead. The Calzone is a work of culinary art, and the pizzas are cooked to perfection, in fact the food is good all round. However, you might want to avoid some of the stranger specials – ostrich anyone?. Be sure to check out the sweet menu though, the tirimisu is to die for.
Mon-Sat: 12-2pm/6-11pm, Sun: 6-10.30pm.
Pollo a la Dino £8.25 HW £8.40

Est Est Est
31-33 East Parade 246 0669
Another chain restaurant but this one has some character. A bright and open layout ensures you're not sat on top of other diners during your visit. The menu is more interesting than you might expect with other options besides pizza and lasagne, although the portions are a bit petit. Always busy, so it's no surprise that booking is advisable during the weekend.
Mon-Fri: 12-2.30pm/5-10.30pm, Sat: 12-11pm, Sun: 12-2.30pm/5.30-10pm.
Fusilli con Pollo (Chicken and Pasta) £6.55, HW £10.25 per bottle

Flying Pizza
Street Lane 266 6501
If you're from Leeds you'll have heard about the Flying Pizza, it's been going for years and is a regular favourite amongst the Roundhay elite. I personally don't think the place is that magnificent to look at, but the food has to be the best I've tasted outside of Italy. The menu ventures beyond the obligatory pizza/pasta delivering some tasty treats in traditional Italian style. The waiters are particularly welcoming, especially to the ladies (no tongues next time, yeah?). This place also acts as celeb watching territory …..ooohhh is that Jimmy Saville over there?
Mon-Wed: 12-2.30pm/6-11pm. Thur-Sat: 12-2.30pm/6-11pm. Sun: 12.30-

3pm/6-11pm.
Saltimbocca Al Romana **£8.90 HW £9.90**

The Italian Job
Bridge End 242 0185
No space to park the mini outside, but the size of portions and the quality of the food means you might need the walk home anyway. On the fringe of Leeds centre, it's well worth a detour to sample the traditional Italian menu. The Spaghetti Aribiata is a must, as is the Tortellini.
Mon-Sat: 12-2.15pm. 6-10.30pm seven days.
Pasta Bolognese £5.00 HW £7.95 per bottle

Pasta Romagna
Albion Place 245 1569
If you live in Leeds you will no doubt have heard the unmistakable loud Opera music booming from this small café/restaurant. The seating outside during the day offers a unique place to stop mid shop and savour a drink or meal. If you'd prefer to eat inside make sure you don't light up in the non-smoking area - Mrs Walker, the loud, Italian matriarch will let you, and the entire population of Leeds, know you're being naughty - the best hangover cure I've found yet. Cheapish, quick and pretty average grub.
7.30am –6.30pm seven days.
Spaghetti Napoleatani £4.50 HW £2.25 per glass

Pizza Express
Crown Street 246 5207
Park Square West 244 5858
Street Lane, Roundhay 268 4509
The way to decide which of these restaurants to choose is to decide on the atmosphere you require. If it's noisy and informal try the Crown St branch (apologies to the staff for always turning up at 11.30pm). For a quieter, more intimate dinner, the other branch is more suited. The food in both is as you'd expect - good pizzas (is it me or are they getting smaller?) and salads in pleasant surroundings. At time of going to press a

third restaurant was about to be unveiled a little further afield in Roundhay.

11.30am-12pm seven days.
Fiorentina Pizza £6.40, HW £10.95

Salvo's
115 Otley Road 275 5017

Salvo's has been dishing up pizzas and pasta dishes for thirty years and haven't they done well? The atmosphere is relaxed and the food very good but you can't book, and the bar is far too small to accommodate the masses of locals and students who regularly tuck in. A small drawback owing to its popularity but don't let it put you off. An unpretentious and lively atmosphere prevails.

Mon-Sat: 12-2pm/6-10.45pm (open 5.30pm Fri/Sat).
Sedani al anitra (pasta with caramelised red onion, tomato sauce and a julienne of barbary duck and Italian sausage roasted with black vinegar £7.50, HW £8.95

Indian

Darbar
Kirkgate 246 0381

Imagine my surprise when the deceptively small doorway opened up onto real palms, decorative fruits and breezy fans. And imagine theirs when I ordered 100 pints of lager and twenty poppadoms. It's really not that kind of place. Unlike the post-pub cheap grub fare usually dished up in these places, the food here is outstanding, and in mammoth portions. Staff are attentive and fantastic. Next time, I'm going in sober.

12pm-2.30pm/6pm-12pm.
Murgh Lahori £9.75, HW £9.50

Elephant Garden
Merrion St 243 9352

New, informal, not very typical Indian in the north end of the city, with chilled out management and clientele enjoying some pretty good curries. It's worth popping over to sample, especially if you're en route to Mojo which is a popadoms throw from Elephant. Wacky bar design and not a Bollywood theme song to be heard.

Mon-Thurs: 5.30pm-12am, Fri/Sat: 5.30pm-3am. (20% NUS discount Mon-Thurs).

Nafee's
69 Raglan Road 245 3128

Smack bang in the middle of

FIND THE NEAREST CASHPOINT ON YOUR WAP PHONE
wap.itchycity.co.uk

www.itchyleeds.co.uk

Studentsville, Nafee's has a reputation for very good food at very good prices, which is funny, because I can only remember really crap curries and the feeling that I've been diddled. The saving graces are that it's always open late, has a very lively atmosphere (jam packed with pissed students) and they let you buy beer takeouts 'til all hours. But not free curries. I've seen what happens to students who try runners from here, and I'm surprised they didn't end up in a Korma.

Mon-Thurs: 12pm-3am, Fri-Sat: 12pm-4am, Sun: 6pm-2am.
Chicken Tikka Masala £6.20 Pint £2.50

Shabab
2 Eastgate 246 8988
A more upmarket version of the Indian restaurants to be found around town but still appealing to a few of the pissheads at the weekend. You should really visit here sober in order to appreciate the quality of Indian cuisine. Curry connoisseurs are welcome.

Mon-Fri: 11.30-2.15pm, Mon-Sat 6-11.45pm.
Muragh Balti £6.90 Hose Wine £7.90

Tariq's
St Michael's Road 275 1881
Been on the lash in spectacular fashion at the Oak/Skyrack? You'll be stopping off at Tariq's then, for an unnecessary, but damn fine meal, which you will no doubt be seeing again in the morning. Shame – the food's worth trying to keep down.

Tues-Thur: 6-2.30am, Fri/Sat 6-3am, Sun: 6-12.30am.
Chicken Bhuna £3.40 HW £6.50

Chinese

Canton Flavour
The Headrow 246 8860

The closest Leeds comes to 'Yo Sushi' atmosphere and service. Take a break from shopping or drinking to witness the fastest food in the East. Canteen style décor may put you off but once you're seated and eating you'll change your mind. Lunchtimes enable you to select your required dish, pay, and wait for it to arrive, whereas the usual restaurant etiquette prevails in the evening.

Mon-Sat: 11.30-9pm, Sun: 12-7pm.
Canton Special Fried Rice £4.90 HW £6.50

Galaxy 105 — THE NEW MIX FOR YORKSHIRE

Lucky Dragon
Templar Lane 245 0520
The Lucky Dragon has gone the full Chinese, complete with red dragons and over-the-top gold trimmings. During the day I've seen staff lugging armfuls of healthy food into the place, which probably explains the heavenly food on offer here. Ever popular and ever so good
12pm-12am seven days.
Stuffed Bean Curd with Prawn meat £7.50, Glass of lychee £1.30

New Jumbo
Vicar Lane 245 8547
Cantonese food experts, providing good food in one of the oldest restaurants of its type in Leeds. Expect to rub shoulders with the luvvie crowd, as it's a stones throw from The Grand Theatre.
12pm-12am seven days.
Fried Sing Chow Style Vermicelli £6.00.

28 28 Chinese Buffet Menu Restaurant
Gower Street 242 6174
Tucked away in the far north of the city, 28 28 seems to do a pretty healthy office workers trade, especially for their lunch buffet. In fact, there's no waiting time here; buffets are all they do – the place doubles up as a training college for future oriental chefs, so, presumably, the contents of the buffet are the result of the days tasks. Sound like a bit of a gamble? Go and check it out, guinea pig.
Tues-Sat: 12-3pm/ 5.30-11pm, Sun 12-4pm/6-10.30pm.
Dinner- £9.00 per person three courses.
Children under 8 eat for half price.

Maxis
Off Kirkstall Road 244 0589
The exterior of this well known and well-loved restaurant is as ostentatious as any I've ever seen. Don't let this put you off. The interior is authentic as are the staff, who are more than happy to explain exactly what each dish is if you're unsure of what to order. And unless you've culinary knowledge matching Egon Ronay, you might well need it with such an extensive menu. Once it arrives - very promptly - it's obvious that these guys know what they're doing. The finest Chinese meal I've had for a long time.
12pm-11pm.
Fried Squid with ginger and spring onion £8.60, Chinese tea £1.10

Japanese

Fuji Hiro
Merrion Centre 243 9184
Sit down and take in the clean lines and décor in this miniature marvel. Food is served quickly, with a smile, and doesn't disappoint. Sample the Japanese and Chinese menu and I guarantee you'll return. They don't take credit cards, and

yes, they know it's the 21st century, and no, they won't make an exception, even for me.
Mon-Thur: 12-10pm, Fri/Sat: 12-11pm.
Yaki Soba (Pan fried noodles with chicken, prawns and seasonal vegetables) £5.50

Little Tokyo
Central Road 242 9090
Very new little Japanese canteen joint, located opposite the rear entrance to House of Fraser with exceptionally friendly staff and, without meaning to reinforce a stereotype, one of the most efficient eating experiences to be had in the city. The bento box set meal houses a healthy cooked meal in a pretty groovy wooded box, prices range from £8.35 – 11.85 There is also an excellent sushi selection that is as much a feast for the eyes as the belly (check out the orange caviar). Definitely a place to try out.
Mon-Sat: 11.30pm-10pm (until 11pm Fri/Sat). No smoking. No alcohol licence.
Nigiri Set (12 sushi pieces) £8.50.

Shogun Teppenyaki
Granary Wharf 245 1856
Absolutely wonderful surroundings for a contender to the best oriental food in the city. Daytimes see the local suit brigade tuck in to sushi and light dishes from the (oh-so-cool) conveyor belt, where you just pick up a dish as it trundles past your eyes, while in the evenings you are treated to your own personal chef, who seems to do a little dance routine, clatters his knife on the table, and presents you with the freshest food you've eaten in a long time. It's not the cheapest place in the world, but if you want to save money, you could always take your partner to McDonald's.
6-11pm, Tues-Sun.
Dover sole fillet with julienne asparagus, mange-tout and white wine, £14.95. HW, £13.00.

Tampopo
South Parade 245 1816
Offering dishes from pretty much everywhere in South East Asia (Japan, Indonesia, Thailand…consult an atlas), this informal canteen style independent chain has you sitting down on square-bum benches and eating good value fodder in pretty minimal, but social surroundings. Situated in the financial end of

town, but attracting a broad spectrum of relaxed diners. 'Food on the go' is the idea, and they can turn around certain cooked dishes in three minutes in the open kitchen. Set two-course lunch menu from £5.50.
Mon-Sat: 12-11pm, Sun: 12-10pm.
Prawns and Basil £9.75, HW £6.50

Teppanyaki

Belgrave Street   245 3345
If you're after a bit of a hullabaloo, here is the place. Teppanyaki is the culinary art indicative of good Japanese cuisine. Here, as is tradition, your food is prepared and presented before your very eyes. The sushi and sashimi are amongst the best in Leeds and as for the tempura (fish coated in a light batter and fried for a few seconds), well, try for yourself. You won't be disappointed. The whole experience is massively entertaining, the final product very satisfying and the service excellent.
Mon-Fri: 12-2pm/6-11pm. Sat: 6-11pm.
Californian Maki (Prawn, avocado and cucumber in a rice roll) £8.00, HW £9.90

Thai

Mai Thai

Lower Briggate   243 1989
Bit of a grotty one this, but the food isn't really that bad and it is pretty cheap.
Mon: 6-10.30pm, Tues-Sat: 6-11pm.
Chicken green curry £5.50 HW £8.50

Sala Thai

Shaw Lane, Headingley   278 8400
This is one of my favourite restaurants in Leeds, and though it takes you a while to find, it's well worth seeking out. All the waiting staff wear traditional dress and are very accommodating, but the real praise goes to the food which is superb. It's not cheap but then quality does come at a price.
6-10.30pm.
All set menus £16.00 per head, HW £7.95 per bottle

Thai Siam

68 New Briggate   245 1608
A fabulous restaurant situated at the North end of the city serving the best in Thai cuisine. For those not too familiar with the world of Thai, sampling one of the set menus here will ensure you become a devotee for life, and once you've found your dish, you'll become a creature of habit. The staff are charming and are eager to help out if you get stuck for choice.
6-11, Tues-Sat, 6-10.30pm Sunday.
Kaeng Ped Phed Yang (duck in a red curry paste) £6.95 HW £8.95

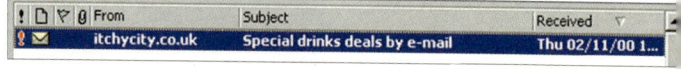

Mexican

Cactus Lounge
St Peter's Buildings 243 6553

If you're partial to a bit of salsa, or frequent the theatre, then you'll no doubt be familiar with this gem. Housed next to Yorkshire Dance and opposite the West Yorkshire Playhouse, this is a shining example of eating in style. The interior is clean, crisp and unassuming, leaving the food to do the talking. The seating is a little unconventional, but comfortable enough and easy to forget once your food arrives. Fajitas to rival those made in Cancun and a delicious vegetarian selection makes the walk to this culinary delight all the more pleasurable.
Mon-Fri: 12-3pm, Mon-Sat: 5-11pm.
Black bean cakes, pan fried with coriander cream and salad and rice £6.70, HW £8.45

Cuban Heels
Assembly Street 234 6115
(See Cafe/Bars)
Mon-Sat: 12-11pm (until 10.30pm Sun).

Caliente Café
Otley Road, Headingley 274 9841
One for those in the know about Mexican food, and judging by the number of bodies in here at any one time, that constitutes the entire population of Leeds. Good-sized portions of the usual Mexican staples are served up to a friendly crowd - they have to be friendly considering the distance, or lack of, between the tables. If you're looking for a good time in a relaxed informal venue, this is the one. There's a no smoking policy in force, but you can always step outside where you'll meet all your nicotine cohorts, trying to grab a few puffs mid-course.
Wed-Sun 6.30-10pm.
Chicken Enchilada £7.95, HW £7.45

```
------- ITCHY INFO -------

WHAT:
 [FRENCH RESTAURANT]
WITH:
 [OUTSIDE SEATING]
NEAR WHERE:
 [TRAIN STATION]
    *SEARCH

OPTIONS                BACK
```

Galaxy 105 THE NEW MIX FOR YORKSHIRE

Spanish

Amigos
70 Abbey Road, 228 3737
Church Walk, 243 5477

A short way out of town stands the best tapas bar in Leeds. So Spanish, you can taste the sangria in the air. All the waiters are truly Spanish (or doing spot-on impressions at any rate), and the food is so magnificent that I regularly rummage through the kitchen bins for leftovers. OK, not quite, but well worth the bus fare and while you're there, you can visit Kirkstall Abbey. There's also a branch in the city centre.
Mon-Sat: 5.30pm – 11pm.
Entremeses variados (Spanish cured meats) £4.95 HW £7.95

La Comida
7-8 Mill Hill 244 0500

At the dodgy end of town, by the train arches, you could be forgiven for overlooking this little restaurant and actually, it might be an idea if you did. The food takes a while to arrive and the wine is a little on the acidic side.
Mon-Sat: 12-3pm, Mon-Sun: 5pm-11.30pm.
Paella £11.50 HW £8.50

La Tasca
Greek Street 244 2205

This place is always packed, day or night - surely the best advert for a restaurant. The wait for a table is worth it though, as this chain actually serves decent food. A comprehensive menu of small but perfectly formed tapas and huge portions of paella keep the punters coming in thick and fast. Large parties are usually seated downstairs - a treat if you like dining in more intimate surroundings.
12-11.30pm seven days.
Paella Marisco £8.50 HW £9.45

Vegetarian

Hansa Gujarati
North Street 244 4408

Fortunately we have here an enlightened proprietor who has realised vegetarians require a little more choice than lentil curry and boiled rice. The choices here are bewildering and no flesh in sight - a welcome change, and recognised as one of the best vegetarians in the region.
Mon-Sun: 6-10.30pm.
Bhagat Muthiya (Chick pea koftas with potatoes) £5.95, HW £7.95

Other / fusion

Art's
Call Lane 243 8243

This culinary delight has gone from strength to strength over the last few years. Once housed in our café bar section, the diversity of its menu means it deserves a mention here. Choose from several Mediterranean dishes on offer as well as a dizzying array of sandwiches, snacks and appetisers. The prices are rea-

---

☥ THE INDEPENDENT The best writers, the sharpest opinions

www.itchyleeds.co.uk

...onable and the atmosphere convivial-ry a lunchtime special for £5.00, and check out some excellent artwork by the manager's brother on the walls.
Mon-Sat: 12-2.30pm, Tues/Thurs: 7pm-2am, Wed-Sat: 7pm1am.
Marinated Lamb chump with parsley mash, rosemary and olive oil jus £9.00, HW £8.00

Artemis
Market Street 243 3737
Lovely little place serving genuinely authentic cuisine. The staff are friendly and are always willing to offer sugges-tions. Traditional music played throughout the week, but no plate smashing sadly (go on, try, and see what they say).
Mon-Sat: 12-2.30pm, Tues/Thurs: 7pm-2am. Wed/Fri/Sat 7pm-1am.
Meze £14.95 HW £8.95

Brasserie 44
The Calls 234 3232
OK, we confess - we haven't actually been to this restaurant. It's too bloody expensive. The food's probably marvel-lous and justifies the price, but we could-n't tell you. Sorry.

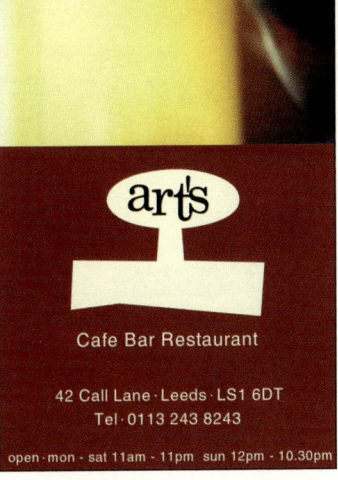

art's
Cafe Bar Restaurant

42 Call Lane · Leeds · LS1 6DT
Tel · 0113 243 8243

open · mon - sat 11am - 11pm   sun 12pm - 10.30pm

Mon-Fri: 12-2pm, Mon-Thurs: 6-10.30pm, Fri-Sat: 6-11pm.
Two courses for £29.50 including sum-mer salad and Herbed noisette of English lamb, Jurancon 1996- Domaine Castera - £15.75 per half bottle.

Dimitris
Dock Street 246 0339
A great place that is set in the trendy part of Leeds alongside all the apartment developments. Once inside, you can imagine being on one of the Greek islands supping Ouzo and gorging on falafel, but alas you're not. There are some mouthwatering seafood dishes on offer or if you're not that hungry you can snack on tapas.
11am-12am seven days.
Stefado £8.95 HW£10.95

THE INDEPENDENT
THE INDEPENDENT ON SUNDAY

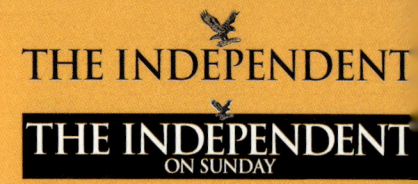

why not subscribe and save over 60%

For a limited period only, The Independent would like to offer you the chance to purchase The Independent & Independent on Sunday for only £1.50 a week, with our advanced purchase payment subscription. Payments can be made by simply telephoning

0800 783 1920

quoting REFERENCE IS01000ITCHY

Offices open Mon to Fri 9am - 9pm, Sat & Sun 10am - 4pm

Answer machine at all other times.

When the application has been processed - which may take up to three weeks - The Independent will send you your fully pre-paid vouchers, which can be used at any news outlet. Alternatively, if you prefer home delivery, please let us know the details of your local participating newsagent (including address and postcode) and we can organise the rest! Your newsagent may charge a nominal fee for this service.

Oporto
Call Lane 245 4444

Famed food in this beautiful restaurant highly regarded for its fish menu which changes daily. It's possible to eat in the bar area but the real story happens next door where the a la carte menu holds court. The prices aren't cheap but the results are more than worth a couple of extra quid.

Mon-Thurs: 12-10pm, Fri-Sat: 12-0.30pm.

Roast cod, saffron mash potatoes and dill sauce £9.95 including starter (12 until 10.30pm (until 6.00 on Saturdays). HW £9.50

TOP FIVE... Cheap Eats
1. Kadas
2. Grove Café
3. Stick Or Twist
4. Normans (Mondays)
5. Citrus

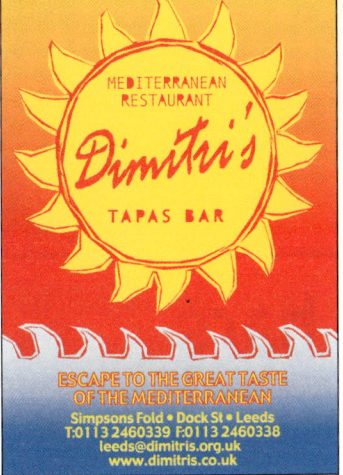

MEDITERRANEAN RESTAURANT
Dimitri's
TAPAS BAR

ESCAPE TO THE GREAT TASTE OF THE MEDITERRANEAN
Simpsons Fold • Dock St • Leeds
T:0113 2460339 F:0113 2460338
leeds@dimitris.org.uk
www.dimitris.co.uk

Velvet
11 Hirsts Yard 242 5079

As well as providing a good atmosphere for drinking, Velvet also caters for those with a passion for food. The upstairs restaurant features chandeliers and balconies all set off by the ever-changing artwork adorning the walls. The bar's known as a gay venue, but that shouldn't prevent people of any sexual orientation sampling the food, and to be honest it isn't overtly gay; they'll welcome people of any persuasion. Expect to book towards the end of the week.

Mon-Sun, 12-10pm.

Shredded duck with pancakes, salad and hoi sin sauce £10.25 HW £10.95

Galaxy 105 THE NEW MIX FOR YORKSHIRE

restaurants

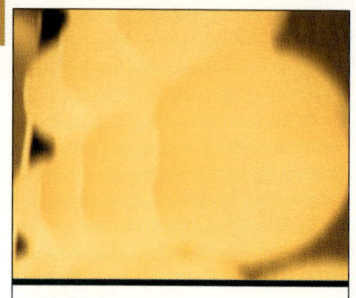

bars

www.itchycity.co.uk

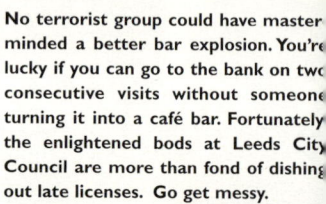

No terrorist group could have master minded a better bar explosion. You're lucky if you can go to the bank on two consecutive visits without someone turning it into a café bar. Fortunately the enlightened bods at Leeds City Council are more than fond of dishing out late licenses. Go get messy.

All Bar One
Greek St 288 2621
In the heart of the financial district stands this bastion of suit-tastic drinking. Alongside lawyers, accountants and other vermin, you'll find suitably dressed secretaries looking to snare a rich husband (who end up chatting up postroom boys with their best suit on). Evenings see a slightly more mixed clientele eager to have a quietish drink before running the gauntlet of city centre bars.
Mon-Sat, 12pm-11pm. Sun, 12pm-11pm.
Marinated chicken in pesto £5.25.

FEEL THE PRESENCE
JOSETTE SIMON, ACTOR.
MORGAN'S SPICED
A MELLOW MIX OF SPIRIT AND SOUL.
THAT FLAVOURS WHATEVER IT TOUCHES.

Atrium

Grand Arcade 242 6116

A three floored palace of sophisticated pleasure Open 'til 2am as a club as well (see club section), but get in before 10 if you want to avoid the door tax, which is quite hefty at the weekend (£5-7). Early bird meal deal, two courses for a fiver.

Open for food 6pm-11pm.
Main club/bar open 'til 2am.

Bar 38

The Headrow 245 6796

For some reason '38' is reminiscent o one of Sonia's album covers. Gold and turquoise has never done it for me. If you can live with the slightly garish brass sur roundings and lack of atmosphere, you're possibly very pissed, but this big ol' brew ery bar is for you. Quieter during the day with a less than inspirational menu. The unisex toilets upstairs aren't the haven o Ally McBeal antics you might expect more long queues and blokes pissing on the seats. On the plus side, it has some pretty cool fountain-come-sink thing in the basement and serves up some 'bet ter than a kebab' cuisine until 2am.

Open 'til 2am, Thurs, Fri, Sat.
Sticky golden chicken £3.45.

LÉ BEFITRUTE CAFE BAR

NEW BRIGGATE   LEEDS   246 9444

LIVE LIFE IN COLOUR

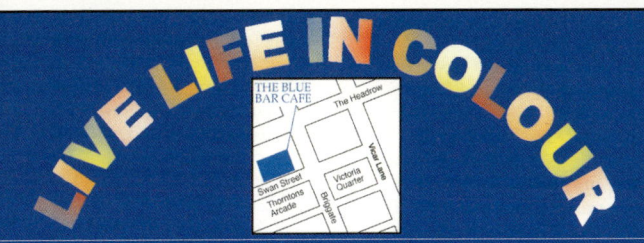

THE • BLUE • BAR • CAFE

Continental Beers • Quality Wines & Champagnes
Full Range of Coffees & Teas • Exciting Menu
Late License • Private Parties Catered For

Swan Street • Leeds • LS1 6JG

Le Beatrute
New Briggate 246 9444

Recently refurbished, with plush new comfy seats, a candle-lit cream and chocolate interior, and a strong line in entertainment, this friendly, relaxed bar at the far north end of the city has a new lease of life. Open 'til 2am six nights, with motown and northern soul (Tues/Wed/Sat), dance (Mon/Fri) and live urban jazz on Thursday. I think the loyal locals are gonna lose their seats to eager new punters coming for the party atmosphere. Their ambitious plans even extend to heaters outside to warm the queues – so take note all you club owners! New menu featuring Mediterranean dishes, their ever tasty hot sarnies and new cocktail range. Smart casual dress, non-members charge after 11pm Mon/Tues (£3), Fri/Sat (£5).
Mon-Sat, 12pm-2am.
Ciabatta insalatta, £3.60.

Blue Bar
Swan St 244 9130
Great location for this up and coming choice of the more discerning Leeds

FIND THE NEAREST CASHPOINT ON YOUR WAP PHONE
wap.itchycity.co.uk

bars

lad/lass. Bright, open plan décor with ample room to sit down (plus covered seating outside in the alley) and enjoy drinking or eating until late. Plans for DJs in the evenings were afoot at time of going to press. See venue for details.
Open until 1am – Thurs, Fri, Sat.
Cajun chicken and bacon wrap, £6.95.
Serves food 'til 7pm.

Café Inseine

Boar Lane 242 2436
Breathe in as you enter this very slim bar on two levels. The plush seating more than makes up for the fact that the queue for the bar tends to interrupt your conversations. Chatty staff and great music on a Friday when the lovely Toby gets on them there decks make this a good bar in which to kick off your night. Well situated for quiet outside drinking in the summer. Food served daily until 7.45 during the week and 6.45 at weekends.
Open 'til 2am Thursday- Saturday.
Chicken, mozzarella and chive sandwich, served hot, £3.75.

Casa

Greek St 224 0005
Serving the local suit population during the day, Casa certainly stands out from the mainstay of brewery owned establishments that tend to be the norm around Greek St. It's a stylish place, very minimal with speakers that resemble loo seats, but this place ain't toilet by any means. Serves 'til 2am on Friday and Saturday and until 12 every other night apart from Sunday, when it's business as usual.
Brie and beef salad, £5.95. Serves 'til 10pm.

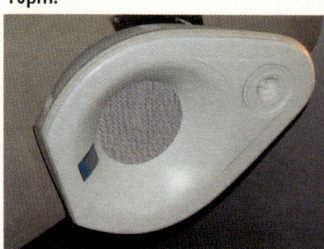

The Courtyard

Cookridge St. 203 1831
Still a place to be seen despite the fact that the centre of 'cool drinking' has moved away from this end of town in the

www.itchyleeds.co.uk

last couple of years. Famous for its heated covered courtyard that stays packed all year round. This bar remains a favourite with relaxed young drinkers as it's one of the few places on this side of town where you can get a late drink without strapping on your heels as no dress code applies. Resident DJ's appear throughout the week playing a mix of soul, garage, r'n'b and funk. Also serves particularly good food.
Serves 'til 2am-Tuesday, Thursday, Friday and Saturday.
Courtyard club sandwich, £3.95.

Cuban Heels
Assembly St   234 6115

Not really enough room to make strapping on your Cuban heels really worthwhile, but it is one of the best bars in the Exchange Quarter, big shoes or not. Not as pretentious as a lot of its neighbours but still attracts the bar butterflies who flit from bar to bar along Assembly Street. DJ's at the weekend make a trip to the bar more hassle than it should be.
Nachos, £3.95. Serves food 'til 10pm.

Elbow Room
Call Lane   245 7011

Food, pool and booze. Heaven! Still packing 'em in since its launch two years ago, this haven of darkness is a great alternative to the usual drinking and more drinking lark. Not like any pool hall you've ever been to (unless you've been to the ones in London) it's more like a club or bar that just happens to have a shit load of pool tables dotted around the place. A 2am licence means you don't have to rush your pint or your game. They've recently had a refurb, so it's looking shiny, and they've plans to open a cocktail and champagne bar to attract a more sophisticated pool shark. Wednesdays sound enticing with the arrival of the East Village Café; expect some of the most eclectic mid-week nights out with great music and free pool.
Classic burger, £5.95. Serves 'til 1.30am.

"The Coolest place to play pool"
(Elle Magazine) - just got cooler.

NEW Cocktail Bar
NEW VIP Lounge
NEW Refurbishment

The Elbow Room
POOL LOUNGE AND BAR.

Facilities now include:

- 15 K-Steel American Pool Tables
- New VIP lounge featuring private pool table, multi-media centre and big comfy sofas, direct phone line to the bar
- New fully stocked cocktail bar with extensive menu
- Waitress service
- TV screen tower showing major sporting events
- Live DJs
- Char-grill menu
- Nightly drinks offers

For private hire of the brand new **VIP** lounge or for any further private hire enquiries please call us on the number below.

The Elbow Room is open every day from midday until 2am Monday-Saturday, 10:30pm Sunday

For information visit our website: www.elbow-room.co.uk

Alternatively you can call us on 0113 245 7011 // The Elbow Room 64 Call Lane, Leeds LS1

Elemental

The Corn Exchange 244 3906

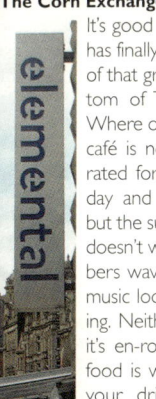

It's good to see that someone has finally decided to make use of that grand space in the bottom of The Corn Exchange. Where once was a quaint little café is now a cool bar, highly rated for its design and open day and night. It looks great, but the sunken dance floor just doesn't work - the happy clubbers waving their arms to the music look like they're drowning. Neither does it help that it's en-route to the loos. The food is worth a go but make your drinks last as they're above average price.

Tapas, £6 for 12. Serves 'til 2am.

Fat Cat Café

South Parade 245 6288

I'm not sure why, but this place seems to attract a bizzarely geeky clientele; there's no Star Wars video games or Who Wants to be a Millionaire machine but they still seem quite happy here. Other than the food, which is pretty good value, there really is no reason to drink here.

Chicken quesadilla £3.95. Normal pub times apply.

Fibre

Lower Briggate 0870 1200 888

Bran' new club that's sure to attract a regular crowd. Fibre looks like a venue that could do very well indeed in Leeds. Right in the heart of Leeds' gay village, Fibre provides Yorkshire with what the Manchester gay scene has enjoyed for so many years. A contemporary food menu served daily from 11am 'til 11pm, whilst at night it's a full on party with resident and guest DJ's playing a mix of 'funky house' and 'essential dance anthems' (perhaps they've booked dangerous Dave Pearce). This is apparently the first phase of the company's move to Leeds, a 1000 capacity club is in the pipeline, plus a retail store and health club - sounds like a whole empire in the making. A predominately gay venue but as long as you don't act too macho, you'll be cool.

Afternoon tea served daily between 1pm and 5pm includes sandwiches, tea or coffee and a scone with clotted cream and preserves, £6 per head.

Mon-Fri 11am-11pm, Sundays 'til 10.30

THE INDEPENDENT ON SUNDAY The best coverage of news & sport

bars

35

Hakuna Matata
Café Bar

SWINEGATE LEEDS TEL: 0113 243 3586

Kombine & Greg Clark

(Space, Liquid, Norman)

dropping all things funky

Soul 2 Funk 2 Hiphop 2 Beatz

Every Friday & Saturday night 9-2

No door charge

Drinks offers: 2 4 1 Mon-Thurs 5-7pm
Fri 4.30pm-8pm

OPEN Mon-Thurs 12-11
Fri 11-2 Sat 5-2

Fudge
Assembly St 234 3588

Teeny tiny place with a huge personality. I know that sounds really shit, but it's a fact. Hosts one of the best day/night events in Leeds - The Vibe - that has taken Sundays by storm since it's arrival in March. An absolute must for anyone who appreciates a music-inspired Sunday communal come-down. No food and no late licence, but if you're not hungry and it's before 11pm, this place is worth an hour of your time, if only to marvel at the design of the loos.

Hakuna Matata
Lower Briggate 243 3586

The exchange quarter hoardes seem to have a major problem with distance. This place is about two minutes walk from Call Lane but is certainly not made the most of. As far as I'm concerned it should stay that way. You can get straight to the bar, they play decent tunes, they're open 'til 2 from Thursday to Saturday and there's not a single Lion King reference in the place, thank God.

Food 12-2, 5–10pm. Closed Sundays.
Warm chicken and pasta salad, £5.95.

www.itchyleeds.co.uk

Henry's
Greek St 245 9424

The 'no trainer' policy gives an indication of the clientele - and you'd be right. Separate eating area and waitress service (even for drinks) makes this a pretty good place to grab some grub but I wouldn't spend a night here and, to be honest, neither should you.
Salmon fillet, £8.25. Serves 'til 5.00pm.

LS One
The Headrow 245 8842

Just because it's housed under the library, don't expect to find any literary types. In fact I'd be surprised if anyone in here has anything fatter than Mr Topsy-Turvy in their book collection. Uninspiring to the point that the only thing that stands out in the memory is the fact that the awning's always covered in bird shit.
8oz Rump steak, £6.95. Serves 'til 6pm.

Mezze
Call Lane 242 9009

TOP FIVE... Late Drinking
1. Oslo
2. Norman
3. Le Beatrute
4. Oporto
5. Townhouse

Another bar that's undergone a bit of a transformation, changing from Soho to Mezze (it's pronounced Mez–ay, by the way). Attracts the same chilled out drinkers throughout the week and handles the Norman overflow at the weekend. The layout is pretty much the same, small but quirkily decked out, but it's much lighter which means you can actually see what you're drinking or who you're snogging, which isn't always a good thing. UK garage on a Sunday.
Tapas served 'til 8pm.

Milo
Call Lane 245 7101

If there is a place in Leeds that has struck the perfect balance between chilled out cool and genuinely friendly atmosphere, Milo is it. Kick back and relax during the week, in anticipation of the blow out weekend in store. The music policy at the weekend ranges from hip-hop through to country rock and you'd be surprised but the dancefloor just ain't big enough. Interesting…
Open 'til 2am Fri/Sat

Telecabs Taxis 0113 231 9000
www.telecabs.co.uk

bars

NORMAN

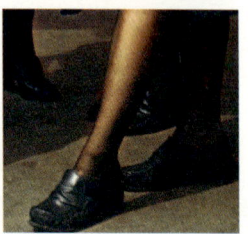

COME AND MEET THE FAMILY

RESTAURANT BAR 36 CALL LANE LEEDS
late licence

Moderno

165 Briggate
234 0301

Art-fuelled café bar with a strong line in cultured antics, from poetry evenings to live jazz. Daytimes are the time to grab a tasty sandwich and a coffee downstairs, or check out the excellent art hangings over lunch upstairs. Unusual beers, a very chilled atmosphere and a surprisingly low goatee count for somewhere like this. Definitely one of the best places in town to have your own private parties.
Californian Melt, £4.70. Serves 'til 10.30pm.

Mojo

Merrion St 244 6387

I know it makes most blokes sick, but you have got to admire the fancy cocktail juggling antics in this place. Fantastic drinks, 'proper' music with guitars and things and it has the best atmosphere of any bar in

MUSIC FOR THE PEOPLE

the city. It was also the only UK bar outside of London to feature in the The Independent's guide to the best bars in the world, so you can take a proper journalist's word for it. Currently applying for a late licence so you might be reading this there at 1am. If you are, put it down, geek.

No 36

Wellington St 261 7091

More of a pub if the truth be told, 36 serves the local office trade a treat. Good menu of cheapish eats and a small outdoor area, facing Wellington Street. which is good for a few rays and a lung full of exhaust fumes. Not easy to get a seat when the surrounding offices finish for the day, but, together with its neighbour, Wharf Street, probably one of the best places in town to catch secretaries off-guard on Fridays at 5.30.
Pork and herb sausage with red onion mash, £4.95. Serves 'til 2.30pm.

Norman

Call Lane 234 3988

Why? I suppose it's better than Darren. Don't look for this place by name as it hasn't got a sign - you should know where it is. Cool cats and hip chicks hang at this designer's dream of a bar. Sit back and count the number of Prada shoes and Gucci shades. Definitely the place to show off your new Harvey Nicks pur-

bars

chase to an appreciative crowd. Currently opens 'til 2am on Thursdays, Fridays and Saturdays, but hoping to be granted permission to do the same every night. Fantastic noodle menu and dodgy seats, but to be honest, there's rarely a spare one anyway.

Blue Monday offer- food and a beer for £5.50.

North Bar

New Briggate 242 4540

With the best selection of beers this side of Belgium, it's the perfect place to start a career in drinking. Extra spice is added by the fresh young art, and inspired, eclectic music selections. Try the Kwak Beer, which to be appreciated in true Kwak style should be consumed from a Kwak tankard, which you can borrow from the bar in exchange for leaving your shoe as a deposit. Far more relaxed than most of the bars on the other side of town. Top staff, top place. Open until 2am Friday and Saturday and 1am Thursdays.

Tapas £2-3.50.

Oporto

Call Lane 245 4444

Oporto was a catalyst to the bar explosion in the Exchange Quarter, and it's still up there with the best of them. Sample something from the inspirational world menu in the restaurant, or just chill in the bar that's open until two at the weekend. It's not usually as busy as much of the Call Lane rabble and the atmosphere's a bit more chilled. A new late licence means you can drink 'til 2am Thursday-Saturday.

Skewered chicken and peppers with coriander rice, £5. Food served 'til 10pm.

Oslo

Briggate 245 7768

Originally planned as a members bar, all you need to get in now is some well-thought out threads and a look that says 'I'm young, trendy and I've got a fat wal-

www.itchyleeds.co.uk

let'. Once you've made it past the dubious selection process (I had a mate refused entry as he wasn't dressed 'flamboyantly enough') you find yourself in an excellently designed subterranean world (I always think 'cosy cave') with cool little alcoves to feel even more VIPish. Careful not to get up to any mischief though – you are being watched. Waiter service, a speciality coffee menu and food with thought, but check your funds, because you've got to pay to be part of this gang, and it ain't cheap. Particularly good DJs drifting from eclectic funky sounds to groovesome house.

Seafood crumble, £4.00. Food served 'til close.

Parisa
Park Row 244 9209

New kid on the block, which is doing a roaring 'business types' trade but an out and out bore in drinking terms. Expect the now obligatory drinking in a library affair; uncomfortable seating and a very loud clientele. Getting served at the bar is a real struggle, as is finding one of those uncomfortable seats. They do brew their own beer and lager though, which is a bit of a saving grace.

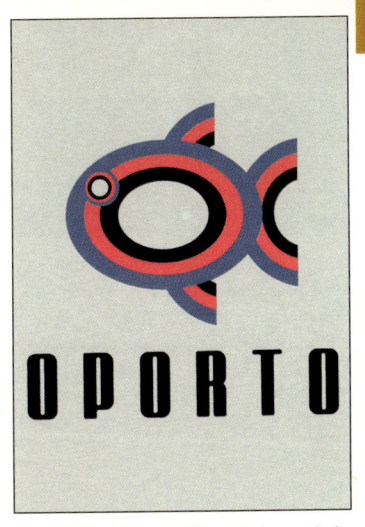

Smoked duck salad, £6.95. Serves food 'til 10.30pm.

Pitcher and Piano
Assembly St 245 7271

Not bad for a chain venture. Good location on the busiest drinking street in Leeds. When the sun occasionally shines the place feels quite Mediterranean, in atmosphere, weather and smell from the sewers. The interior is as you'd expect - wooden floors, grand sofas and floor to ceiling windows; the result is a pleasant enough environment in which to spend a

Galaxy 105   THE NEW MIX FOR YORKSHIRE

bars

few hours. The food is especially good.
Potato wedges with bacon and cheese, £4.00. Food served 'til 9pm.

Quid Pro Quo
Greek St 244 8888

In comparison to its neighbours Quid Pro Quo is looking a little battered, still it's certainly benefiting from the overspill from Casa next door. A popular haunt for the suit brigade, especially on Friday's when it gets particularly busy. I wouldn't be surprised if during the life span of this book this place undergoes a massive refurb - it desperately needs it if it's gonna keep up.

Open 'til 2am Thursday, Friday and Saturday.
Chicken ciabatta, £4.95. Serves food Mon-Wed 'til 9pm, Thurs-Sat 'til 2am.

Revolution
Call Lane 243 2778

Vodka? I should coco. Stacks of flavoured shooters, cocktail pitchers and an excellent range of world vodkas (I'm hooked on Zubrowka Bison). This place really rocks at the weekend with DJs spinning tunes on a hip-hop and R'n'B vibe and a good-sized courtyard with plenty of tables to hang onto after the seventh tipple. It's the only chain bar on a street full of independents, it's less pretentious and

TOP FIVE
Pull (Fussy)
1. Norman
2. Oporto
3. Oslo
4. Elbow Room
5. Space

its emphasis firmly placed on the religion of getting hammered. A fantastic place to worship.
Late drinking 'til 2am Thursday-Saturday.
Club Sandwich, £5.75. Serves 'til 6pm.

Roc Bar
Boar Lane 245 5300
Doesn't really look like a bar from the outside as it merges bizzarely with the pie shop next door. This place is certainly attracting that trendy Leeds lot who have been coming here in droves since it replaced the dodgy La Crème. Get beyond the bakery-like exterior, down to the large basement and there's a bar, good-sized dance floor, and lots of comfy seating. Music is on a housey house tip that suits the mood of its patrons. Lots of talent on offer for you singletons but no pies, unfortunately.
Serves 'til 2am, Mon-Sat. No food.

Rocket
Swinegate 244 1573
If you want shielding from the incessant beat of house music in Leeds, your salvation comes in the form of this gem. Housed under the railway bridge, and with a recent facelift to add to the attraction, it's more than just 'the bit on the edge of The Cockpit'. The Cockpit is home to the now legendary Mod fest of Brighton Beach (along with other more indie-orientated nights) and The Rocket, becomes an annex of the club. Also a recommended gig venue; the Bloodhound Gang, Ooberman and chums have played here. A good place to pull a nice indie lad/lass.
Open 'til 2am every night apart from Sunday. No food.

Soul Kitchen
York Place 242 1202
Slightly off the beaten track is this sparkling example of how eating and drinking should be conducted. Take a seat in the underworld of Soul Kitchen and prepare to be dazzled by an innovative menu, the friendliest staff, and an atmosphere difficult to match. The food on offer ranges from home made wild mushroom risotto (£4.25) to kebabs as well as a fairly new delivery service

find places for late drinks on your WAP phone
wap.itchycity.co.uk

bars

43

aimed at the residents of Leeds' burgeoning loft dwellings. Acts as a pre-club venue to the infamous Speed Queen.

Tequila Tequila

Grand Arcade, Vicar Lane 244 4472

There are numerous Mexican restaurants in and around Leeds, but this is the first Mexican themed bar, and let's be honest, would you rather spend a night with nachos and fajitas or Corona and tequila? You can sit outside and check out the talent on their way to Heaven & Hell and Atrium, shimmy around to latino and hip hop in the upstairs bar, or make your way through the excellent cocktail shooters menu. And with a two-for-one offer until 8pm through the week, it has been our standard starting place for itchy trouble. They've also started serving food from 11am, and with the delicious Pasta Latino at £3.95, it's a bargain.

Open 'til 1, but it may extend that to 2 soon.

Name and occupation?
Richard, recent graduate
Unemployed then. Where do you drown your sorrows? Oslo
Schmooze the ladies? Po Na Na
Where do you hold your cutlery in that same funny fashion? La Tasca
I wouldn't wear those clothes, but if I had to, where could I buy them? French Connection
Leeds, what's hot? It's a compact city
And what's definitely not? The weather

Townhouse

Assembly St 219 4000

Once the jewel in the crown of Assembly Street, it seems to have slipped from grace a little ('Towniehouse' springs to mind), but remains packed 'til 2 on all three floors at the weekend, when it feels more like a club atmosphere. On Saturday afternoons you'll find the Townhouse at it's best, when you can take a seat outside and crane your neck to your hearts content at the passing tal-

Galaxy 105 THE NEW MIX FOR YORKSHIRE

ent. Certainly the most pretentious bar in the area, and probably Yorkshire; if you want to fit in make sure you've got a decent line in talking bollocks and if you don't own a pair of Evisu, get some Tipp-ex to your Wrangler's. Serves a selection of dishes, including fresh soups, salads and sandwiches all for under a fiver, and 'til 2 in the morning, not that you'll have room to eat them.

Velvet
Hirst's Yard   242 5079

Classy place. The menu downstairs ranges from divine sandwiches and soups, right through to anything from the upstairs restaurant menu. The friendly staff are amongst the most attentive I've had the pleasure of meeting (even if a little vain). Gets absolutely packed at the weekend, with DJ's playing a selection of house orientated choons. Rub shoulders with cowboys and angels and other clubbers sporting wonderful regalia as this place acts as a pre-club venue to Speed Queen.
See Gay section
Roast duck and Japanese noodles, £8.95. Serves 'til 10pm.

---

tequila tequila

MEX BITES
PARTIES
TEQUILA
RUM
COCKTAILS
SUNDAY SESSIONS
TEQUILA
CIGARS & TEQUILA

featuring the **cubaroom**

1-3 Grand Arcade, Vicar Lane, Leeds, 0113 244 4472

Find things fast at
www.itchyleeds.co.uk

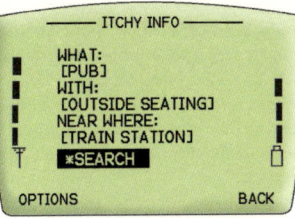

```
--- ITCHY INFO ---
WHAT:
[PUB]
WITH:
[OUTSIDE SEATING]
NEAR WHERE:
[TRAIN STATION]
*SEARCH

OPTIONS                    BACK
```

Find what you want using your WAPphone
wap.itchyleeds.co.uk

Wardrobe

St Peter's Buildings 242 3104
A very New York style bar near the the West Yorkshire Playhouse. Owned by some of Leeds' big entertainments cheeses, it's aimed at the slightly older, more sophisticated crowd, which they generally get, except for when Zack and the young indie looking scruffy kid out of Emmerdale come in, as they tend to lower the tone a little.- see club section for full review.

Headingley

The Arc

Ash Road, Headingley 275 2223
A fantastically welcome and much needed new bar in Job-dodger central. Eating out in Headingley has generally meant Bryans fish and chips or the Oak carvery, but this latest venture has changed all that, offering good pub grub in surroundings that you might expect of an up-market city centre restaurant. A main dish is no more than seven quid and the atmosphere is like nothing you will have sampled before in Headingley – i.e. not packed with the student rugby squad. There's live jazz every Sunday and a cocktail bar selling a choice of over 600 cocktails – whether the staff can remember the correct ingredients remains to be seen.
Pizza Funghi £4.75.

Citrus Pool Bar

North Lane, Headingley 230 2810
New pool hall/bar in Headingley, attracting the young professional and older student market for drinking, chilling and a spot of pool on one of the six US pool tables (but don't embarrass yourself by looking like a lemon). Surprisingly big loft-style interior, especially when you consider the tiny-looking exterior. Members only (don't worry; it's free). Normal pub hours and funky DJs at the weekend. Pool £5 p/h.

Name and occupation?
Anna, Psychology student
Read my mind. I drink at the Townhouse
Spooky. And for… Mint for the best dancing
Blimey. Eating? Yes, yes, Est Est Est, and I shop at Mambo before you ask
Can I… You pervert, piss off

bars

pubs

www.itchycity.co.uk

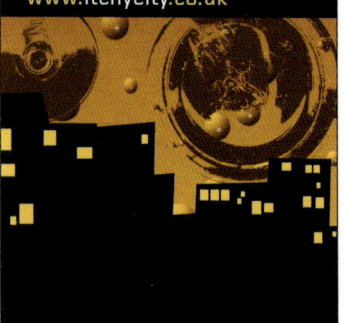

Leeds pubs are more popular than ever. Not everyone longs to drink in a Habitat-style wine bar with Henry, Loretta and their bum chums. There's nowt more satisfying than the wheel of booze landing on your favourite tipple. Go spin...

City centre

Aire

The Calls 203 1811
Slightly quieter since the installation of Bar Central down the road, but still a good place to sit and contemplate life whilst looking out over the river. They do a good lunch menu served 12-7 Thursday-Saturday and 12-3 Monday, Tuesday, Wednesday. Probably one of the best places for summer drinking with seats outside, near to the river.

The Bankers Draft

Park Row 204 8581
This brewery owned pub has just replaced O'Neills, but retains the same feel as before with good seating and a relaxed mood. Serves your typical pub

food menu everyday from 11-7pm. An obvious choice of name really, it's on Park Row with all the banks, and is usually full of 'merchant bankers'.

Big Lil's Saloon Bar
Bramley's Yard   242 3910
Not a fresh face in sight as that hardened drinker complexion is perfected here seven days and nights a week. There are no pretensions here - D&G trollies will not be appreciated, and the pint prices reflect the fact that you won't see anyone else in them - £1 for a pint of John Smiths. Free fights all year round.

Brannigans
Vicar Lane   244 1991

Bucks Fizz played here; tells a story doesn't it? More of the same in this run of the mill, but vast pub/live music venue - don't expect to see Oasis here…not the real ones anyway. Probably accounts for about half of Steps royalty cheques. Best place in Leeds to find that Capri driving sugar daddy, or Dorian from Birds of a Feather look-a-like, to share the mini cab back to Beeston.

Brownes
Gt George St   246 9699
Big, brash drinking den, with oh-so-nineties décor and uncomfy seating. Acts as a sort of pre-bar for the legendary Majestyk, so you know what to expect.

Carpe Diem
Civic Court   243 6264

A cosy little boozer, with lots of comfy seats and hidden away booths, Carpe Diem is a great place to have an intimate drink with your sweetheart. There probably isn't a more convenient place to get absolutely paralytic – it's just down the road from the General Infirmary, and usually packed with trainee doctors and nurses. Weekends see the medics mix with townies as they all act as human tinnitus guinea pigs to a mix of chart and house. Serves 'til one.

The Conservatory
Albion Place   205 1911
This underground bar provides escape during the day, with frazzled shoppers swapping nightmare retail stories. The place is looking a bit battered but it doesn't seem to worry the up-for-it pre Majestyk crowd at the weekend.

Duck and Drake
Kirkgate 246 5806
Bit like that future Eastenders Christmas special when the X-Files lands in Albert Square. Full of unexplained phenomena and Pat Butcher look-a-likes who make little effort to hide their un-earthly origins. Interesting little local, and tasty booze.

Edwards
Merrion St 246 9297
'Are you looking at my girlfriend/mum?' (often one and the same) is the normal banter in this city centre pub. A pity really as the food is actually quite good and the choice of booze on offer extensive. Look out for the special offers, and the flying punches.

Empire Bar
The Headrow 244 4750
Same format as the majority of pubs around this part of town - cheeky décor and cheeky customers. Don't expect anything amazingly different, from the beer to the food. Cheap menu deals though.

Felon and Firkin
Gt George St 244 6263
Fairly student filled. Conversation may deviate from 'what A-levels did you get?' to 'Yeah, but how many times have you removed a spleen?' as it's located next to Leeds General Infirmary. Not a bad venue for the doctors of the future to congregate when they finish their 70-hour shift to reminisce about tonsils and tracheoctomies.

The Grove
Back Row 243 9254
A proper pub. Everything around it may have been knocked down and replaced with huge air-conditioned office blocks, but this oasis of real ale and grot remains. During the day the local office girls and boys come out to play, sign deals or bunk off. There's live music nearly every night including the awesome Wednesday night jams; turn up, bring an instrument and either entertain or irritate, try to avoid the latter as you won't be popular. One of the best real pubs in the city. Leave it alone, big brewery bastards.

The Guildford
The Headrow 246 8635
Walking in here is like stepping back in time. The clientele is old and the decoration older. One to avoid if you're on the pull, unless you like your men very, very, old. Not bad for the footie, if a little cramped.

THE INDEPENDENT ON SUNDAY — The best coverage of news & sport

www.itchyleeds.co.uk

Hogshead
Gt George St, Lower Briggate 244 2275
The big brewery Changing Rooms team have got to this place. They kept that big jessie with long hair away from it so there's no fluorescent medieval water feature in the middle of the bar, more's the pity. Just re-created wooden boozer interior and a host of guest ales. The sarnies bring a whole new meaning to the word doorstep.
Sandwich selection from £3.

Josephs Well
Hanover Walk 203 1634
Fave hangout of the indie/alternative scene, with a fantastic jukebox and a licence 'til 12am throughout the week. They also have some decent local bands performing, and some of the big boys are known to play here. Just the place to find your Kurt Cobain lookalike.

Len's Bar
York Place 244 3590
Cavernous pub up in the financial district, forgotten by many except at knocking off time, when it's rammed with over-paid drinkers trying to save a few quid for their next Louis Vuitton wallet. God knows how they manage to have so many cheap booze deals, but they do. Lots of cosy seating with a cool library ensemble too.

Northern Snooker Centre
Kirkstall Road 243 3015
Proper snooker hall. More tables than you can shake a cue at, an American pool hall upstairs a bar and a restaurant. Ideal location for an afternoon drinking session; find a good table, order the beers, take advantage of the grub and pretend you're Paul Newman in The Hustler.

The Observatory
Boar Lane 242 8641
You can generally get a good picture of a pub/bar by observing the fall out at closing time. If you like your shoes, dress, hair to be intact at the end of the evening maybe this isn't the place for you. Hoards of lager boys and pastel chicks stumbling

Galaxy 105 THE NEW MIX FOR YORKSHIRE

out at the end of the night make this end of town a bit of an obstacle course, be it for their fighting, shouting or snogging. Late licence ensures this old timer keeps ramming them in.

Old Monk

Greek St 243 1808

The nearest to a proper pub on the street, 'The Monk' is a sturdy favourite with the older office workers and postroom boys for a real pint before the short jog to the station. They often have good drinks deals but steer clear of the food; in my opinion it's pretty dire. Shows the football, but on fairly small screens.

Old Royal Oak

Kirkgate

One of the oldest pubs in Leeds and a REAL Irish one at that. Great atmosphere with a largely local, loud, Irish clientele, but generally appealing to an older crowd. Still known as 'Diddly Dee' for its live music. Don't panic if the bloke you're sat next to hasn't moved for twenty minutes - he's probably trying to communicate telepathically with his whippet.

Oscars

Albion St 246 8899

Good place to play pool as there are regular competitions. The real source of entertainment, however, is supplied by the pissed up lads and lasses on their way to Majestyk. Serves good cocktails. Look out for the door next to JJB Sports, and definitely look out for the slippery stairs.

Quo Vadis

The Headrow 243 4172

I do feel sorry for this place, as no one ever seems to be in here. The atmosphere, free from people, is similar to the feeling Cainey must have felt prior to the natives coming over the ridge in Zulu - pensive and desolate. Shame, but its location means it gets no passing trade. Love the big sofas.

Rat and Parrot

Woodhouse Lane 243 6215

Mammoth pub, but a beautiful building nonetheless. Apparently the biggest pub in the country in terms of cubic feet, but most of that is taken up by the aircraft hanger-style roof. Sofas, lots of chairs, substantial bar and good food, in theory

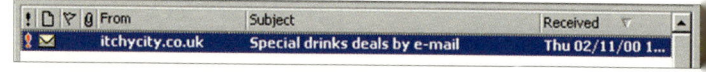

!	🗋	▽	0	From	Subject	Received ▽
👤	✉			itchycity.co.uk	Special drinks deals by e-mail	Thu 02/11/00 1...

www.itchyleeds.co.uk

should make this a great place to start the night. It's OK during the day but is too loud to hear yourself drink in the evenings but it doesn't seem to bother the hordes of Bacardi Breezer drinkin' lasses and lads desperately trying to remember where their mates are sitting.

Scarborough Taps

Bishopsgate 243 4590
Characterful, proper pub, a stone's throw from the train station. Attracts the suit brigade during the day, whilst all manner of people frequent in the evening. Good place to avoid students and actually have a conversation while you drink. Popular as a pre-football venue when Leeds United play at home, especially with away fans.

Sinbin

The Headrow Centre 234 2282
Formerly the bar belonging to Lillywhites, this is another one dominated by all things sporty. Despite being a rugby-based pub there's not too much standing on tables with trousers round the ankles, but maybe I was just in on a good night. Good place to watch all the big matches (it's not too busy – yet) and the food is great too.

Springbok

Woodhouse Lane

Since they banned showing Leeds games in the Walkabout this is the best place in the city to watch the Whites storm to another podium finish in the Premiership. The focus is on rugby really (it's a South African theme bar) but they have tellies everywhere and constantly show sport. Good place to catch the international ten-pin bowling championships.

Square on the Lane

Boar Lane 246 0111
Favourite of the Majestyks and Planet Earth crew, aiming to eye up any potential victims for later in the night. The huge

pubs 53

TOP FIVE... Watch The Footy
1. Original Oak
2. Skyrack
3. Springbok
4. Walkabout
5. Elland Road

queues outside are proof as to how popular this townie bar is. Which in turn is proof that a lot of people have no taste. Enjoyable if you like fat girls in short skirts and avoiding the glare of meatheads looking for a fight.

Stick or Twist
Merrion Way 234 9748
The drink prices are the main reason for visiting this Weatherspoons outfit. Well, they must be - it can't be the music, décor, or regular clientele. Slightly sterile environment, but if you've got a drink in your hand it's not really that important. Right underneath the Grosvenor Casino (hence the name), so you can calm the nerves, then drown your sorrows.

Victoria Commercial Hotel
Great George St 245 1386
A good brewery pub with no nonsense, cheery staff, listed ales, and a real mixture of characters help take you back to what it may have been like in a turn of the century city ale house. This is the sort of place that Americans still think is on every street corner, and in my opinion it would be pretty cool if they were. Beware the ghost!

Walkabout
Cookridge St 205 6500
A favourite with the students, a mere boomerangs throw from the Met. One to avoid on a Wednesday when the place is stuffed with sport teams whose soul purpose is to get absolutely pissed out of their heads and dance to Rolf Harris's 'Two Little Boys'. The best place to watch sport though, with its two giant widescreen pull downs and enough tellies to ensure you cannot hide from getting pummelled by Man U again. Don't expect to watch Leeds though – they're not allowed to show the matches.

The Wellington
Low Road 272 9571
This used to be an Irish style bar, but nowadays it's home to lunching businessmen and is usually dead once they've given up trying to pull their secretaries and gone home to their wives.

Galaxy 105 THE NEW MIX FOR YORKSHIRE

www.itchyleeds.co.uk

The Whip

Duncan St 245 7571

Arguably serves the best pint of Tetley around, this is a proper hard, proper Northern pub. It's pretty dingy and dark inside which doesn't really matter as most people are comatose, staring at John McCririck and his horses on the telly, dribbling into their pints.

Whitelocks

Turks Head Yard 245 3950

Whitelocks is a haven of the traditional in a city that has become increasingly obsessed with all things modern and post-modern. The building itself has existed since the 1700's and many of its features are listed. Good location in the middle of town, so it's perfect for a quick refuel between Harvey Nicks and Habitat. Also serves some good food, if a little on the frugal side.

Yates's Wine Lodge

Woodhouse Lane 245 4928
Boar Lane 244 8566

"A day without wine is a day without sunshine" they proclaim on their walls. Too true. But not spending the day at Yates's is no loss, as it's a bag of toss. Everyone and everything shouts, from the bar staff to the decor. Remember you only have one life, and it's best spent elsewhere.

Headingley/Hyde Park

The Chemic Tavern

Johnson St, Woodhouse 295 0195

A great alternative to the nightmare queues that are typical of pubs further up the road in Headingley. The Chemic Tavern sits in what can only be considered as the nice bit of Woodhouse. Great pub with an unusual atmosphere; locals and students mix peacefully.

Hyde Park

Hyde Park Corner 275 9352

Mr Q's got their grubby hands on this pub, cranked up the volume and laid on a few pool tables. Full of students, old men, football nutters and nutters of the regular variety, who mingle here for a spot of drinking. Big screen sports and ropey but edible food served all day. Loud in the evenings with regular entertainment such as quizzes and karaoke. Entertainment is used in the loosest

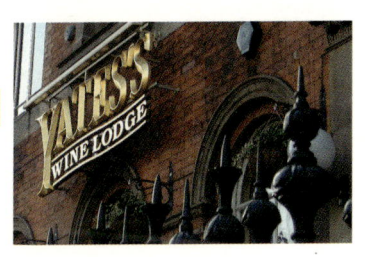

pubs

OTLEY RUN

Hard drinkers drink hard, and never harder than on the Otley Run. Naturally, we don't condone such behaviour, irresponsible drinking and lack of respect for alcohol. But we know people who do, so...

Ground rules: One pint per pub, preferably premium lager although you're allowed two 'spirit breaks', where you may substitute a double spirit for a pint. You must also do a minimum of 13 pubs. Take your time - it's a marathon, not a sprint, and the gob-shite encouraging you to 'drink up you nonce' will invariably be spewing his guts up around the Pack Horse.

Working your way into town:
Woodies, Three Horseshoes, New Inn, (Headingley Taps), Oak, Skyrack, Hyde Park, Library, Pack Horse, Eldon, (University union bar), (Fav), Fenton, Dry Dock, (Met bar) and finish up with the cheesiest club you can find, preferably Ritzy, Heaven and Hell or Majestyk. Let's face it, you're not going to get in anywhere classy.

sense of the word, many would feel punishment to be more appropriate. Seat outside on the fume-choked Otley Road

Headingley Taps
North Lane   230 2493

An inside-out tardis. A huge building with criminally very little of it devoted to the bar area. If you're the type of person who thinks all students do is sponge off the state and spend money on slap up meals, come here to boil your blood a little, because it's full of them. Not a bad place to pull a fresher, watch big-screen sports or do a quiz.

The Original Oak
Otley Road   245 8842

Students are either in here, in bed, or in lectures and let's face it, it's not going to be the latter. Absolutely rammed all the time; self-respecting students spend the majority of their grant here. Football is shown on two or three big screens in this massive three barred boozer. The bowling lawn outside has long been sacrificed as a beer field for summer drinking, which is more than taken advantage of by the real students who nip down to Oddbins for eight Buds for a fiver and try to look innocent as they craftily sup them on the lawn.

Royal Park
Queens Road   275 7494

Big place, does exactly what it says on the door. Frequented by locals and students, the Royal Park ain't the most sophisticated place to drink, but it's better than staying in all night, no? Live bands play in The Cellars from time to time, stacks of pool tables (check out the room upstairs), a Roy Castle non-smoking room and big screen for the football.

Skyrack
Otley Road 275 2123
They've extended it now to Original Oak proportions, attracting a broader crowd than the former rugby-playing, pants down, pissing at the bar, I'm hilarious what what' types. More wooden than their padded-seat rival across the road, this place is massive, with loads of different seating areas. Now home to some free internet points - what were they thinking? So it's now the only place where you can eat your Sunday lunch and see a spit-roast at the same time. Big crowds, big beer garden, big noise and incredibly popular.

University area

Dry Dock
Woodhouse Lane 245 4064
I know, we'll get an old barge, stick a bar and some giant games of Connect 4 in and slap it bang in the middle of a traffic island. And so, after some drug-fuelled fantasy, the Dry Dock ran aground (I reckon the planners in the city council probably enjoyed a little loose juice before they approved it as well). A stone's throw from the Met this place gets rammed with job dodgers during term time and sun seekers out on deck on the odd warm day.

The Fenton
Woodhouse Lane 2453908
No gimmicks in this little student ale house. Good grub, a good pint and conversation from the philosophy students bunking off. Priceless.

The Library
Woodhouse Lane 244 0794
This pub, formerly known as the Feast and Firkin, is now The Library and belongs to the 'it's a scream' chain of boozers. It's your typically recreated olde worlde venue and is within vomiting distance to some of the halls of residence for Leeds Uni students. Obviously renamed for the hilarious gag potential of students going to study down 'The Library'. Stop this now, get a job.

Pack Horse
Woodhouse Lane 245 3980
An old fashioned, local type pub that doesn't get too rammed with students despite its location opposite the University. Excellent place to escape for a game of darts and a quiet pint of Tetley. Watch out for comedy nights in the room upstairs, occasionally featuring John 'boatfoot' Emmerson

pubs 57

clubs

www.itchycity.co.uk

For information about club nights flic to pages 68/69. For up to date reviews previews and listings tap your way to www.itchyleeds.co.uk or on your WAP phone goto wap.itchyleeds.co.uk.

After Dark (Orbit)

The Pavilion, South Green St, Morley 252 8202

The bastion of all things techno and a absolute must if you're in Leeds and lik your beats. The calibre of guests are good enough reason alone to go; Claud Young mixing with his chin, DJ Hell, Je Mills (Oh the bells!), Joey Beltram and C Bolland, but you have to witness the tru

'Morley heads' as they attach their laces to the balconies to prevent themselves from falling off during frantic arm waving sessions. A tenner cab ride out of Leeds but oh so worth it.

The Atrium

Grand Arcade 2426116

For those of you who require a little depth in your late night freakin' and not a whiff of 'Do you come here often?'

Tongue

TWISTER+

FINEST QUALITY GUMMED PAPERS

RIZLA+ It's what you make of it.

www.rizla.com

you'll find that The Atrium offers a lot more than the usual. A bar/café/club in one, its lack of chart music kinda elevates it above some of Leeds' other venues. You're also likely to run into that creative cutie you've been admiring from a distance. A haven for those who can't face tottering amongst the vomiting bods at Majestyk.

Barcelona

Centre 27 Business Park, Batley

Barcelona? My arse! The name might conjure up exotic images of Catalonian passion, but the reality is a big shed in a car park near Batley. If you do trek from the city you will be greeted by a cartoonish interior in garish colours, and that's before you've had a drink. If you like dodgy music and dodgy pulls, then fair enough. If not, you'd be advised to go clubbing as far away from Barcelona as possible. A small Lincolnshire town should be about the right distance.

Club 66

Boar Lane

Formerly Nato, and formerly a decent venue. Judging by the queues outside it's a place for eyeing up the talent and avoiding the inevitable fights with hairspray and teasing combs in the toilets. It's under the soon-to-be obsolete C&A, which might give a further indication of what to expect. If you get bored in there you could always peruse the copious amounts of books in the 'library'.

Cockpit

Swine Gate 244 1573

If you want shielding from the incessant beat of house music in Leeds, your salvation comes in the form of this gem. Housed under the railway bridge, the Cockpit/Rocket bar is home to the now legendary Mod-fest of Brighton Beach, along with other more indie-orientated nights. Also a recommended gig venue - Badly Drawn Boy, Coldplay and chums have played here. Always a good place to pull a nice indie lad/lass.

Digby's

York Place 244 3590

Once the home of the infamous Glasshouse, which has re-located to Heaven and Hell, Digby's has come up with Shattered; a night that is in the same vein, playing the hardest of hard house imaginable. The place for insomniacs who can't face going home at 2am, a maze of a venue, a pub during the day, and a run down chill out area at night.

Hot tip

60   www.itchyleeds.co.uk

Evolution
Cardigan Field Leisure Park, Kirkstall Road 263 2632

Big out-of-town club in a shed conveniently located near studentville. Most nights of the week this place is like Rixon's on the first day of the January sales - big queues of cheaply-dressed people, irritating staff and cheap TV's everywhere. The fact that Tim Westwood plays here does nothing for its credibility either. However, if you like lots of vodka and low cut tops …easy tiger.

The Fav
Springfield Mount 245 8817

When I was at uni, this place was called the Faversham but everyone called it the Fav. The new big brewery owners have listened to the kids and named it so. The place went into decline over the last few years, not able to keep up with the city centre bar explosion. The new owners haven't had much time to turn it round but if they can bring back some of that Fav fever they'll do well. Thursdays sound promising with a mixing competition and free admission, so all those bedroom DJ's out there get amongst it and rock the party.

Fluid
New York St

We were promised that this place was going to be open by October, but we're still waiting, I suppose it all adds to the hype though. Leeds loves its house music, and now we've got another venue playing those repetitive beats to prove its devotion. It's all a bit hush, hush but I'm informed that we can expect great things from the Fluid posse. Apparently they've only gone and got Pav – the live percussionist from Manumission to play there – woweee! It's gonna' be like Ibiza all over again - God help us!

Fruit Cupboard
Call Lane 243 8666

Say goodbye to what was, and welcome the new and greatly improved. I've always liked the Fruit Cupboard but thought there were greater possibilities here at the cornerstone of Call Lane. Thankfully, those jazzy types behind The Space have got behind the club and are set to launch the 'only urban club in Leeds to have its music policy predominantly driven by black music'. That's what they say anyway, and judging by the success of The Space can anyone doubt them?

RIZLA+ It's what you make of it.

The HiFi Club Club/Bar/Food & Live Music
A Soul/Jazz/Funk/Boogaloo/Motown/Latin/Old Skool/Northern And Hip Hop Thing
2 Central Road/Near The Corn Exchange/Leeds/West Yorkshire

Formerly Known As Liquid The Totally Refurbished Venue Features The New And Classic Sounds Of The Much Loved Underground The HiFi Club Is Home To Moveonup/Sunday Joint/Sweet Reviva/Harlem Bush Club/Boogaloo And FunkSoulNation
Telephone: 0113 242 7353/Website: www.thehificlub.co.uk

Fuse (formerly Casa Loco)
Lady Lane (the Chinese Quarter)

Playing uplifting house and garage on Fridays and hard house on a Saturday, Fuse is satisfying the staple diet of the Leeds clubbing population for after hours revelry. The venue, formerly known as Casa Loco, used to be synonymous with bad boys, but seems to have cleaned up its image. Now the only people hassling you are the ones requiring a helping hand remembering their name.

Heaven and Hell
Grand Arcade   243 9963

Another one at which to sport that tight, lime green lycra number you've bee saving. Big, brash and on three leve (Heaven, Hell and Purgatory) the resu rected Pleasure Rooms is the only venu in Leeds to mount a serious challenge t Majestyk's mainstream dominance. Eac floor hosts a variety of music, general commercial dance music and that awfu euro-pop (funnily enough, in 'Hell' down stairs). It's the type of place that you'r likely to hear the crowd making thos ridiculous owl type noises to the beat o the music. Recently featured in Th Sport, when the barmaids showed pun ters their breasts if they spent over £1 on a round. The place was full of peopl carrying four pints around with them a

Flick through the papers

ight. To be honest, unlike the venue, there's no inbetween; you'll either be in heaven or hell, depending on your level of sophistication.

The Hi-Fi Club
Central Road   242 7353

ay hello to the new arrival on Leeds ubbing circuit – The Hi-Fi Club. A fusion of Liquid, the venue which it's set to replace, and The Underground which as sadly closed down at the end of last summer. If you're familiar with any nights that were hosted at either, you'll know what to expect. If you're not, then think zz-soul-funk mixed with a fab set of people minus the ponciness that frequently infests this end of town. Plus the favourite night of the itchy team - Move On Up - is set to be re-born here too.

Majestyk
ity Square   242 4333

nightclubs were amusement parks this would be Blackpool Pleasure Beach and Alton Towers all rolled into one. It's been scientifically proven that it's impossible not to pull in here. Frequented by local Emmerdale celebrities, and made famous on a national scale by brawling Leeds Ltd players (perhaps/allegedly/don't sue, please). Massive place providing cheesy tossed-up revelry to the masses. Occasional jaunts into less commercial ventures prove that Majestyk has the ability to be credible, but pints, not pills, pay the bills.

Mint Club
Harrison Street   244 3168

Tucked away from the hoards of lager lads that populate this end of town, the Mint Club continues to deliver some great nights. This is especially true of the relocation of Stush, which proved to a be a great success at its former home, Nato. Though much smaller than the infamous Pleasure Rooms, Basics occupies the Saturday slot and continues to pack in the beautiful people week after week. Residents Ralph Lawson and James Holroyd are joined by a host of top drawer guests pumping out house-orientated sounds. The Evian-themed garden (garden, in the loosest sense of the

the Mint club

THURSDAYS > STUSH

FRIDAYS > CLEAR

SATURDAYS > BASICS

tel: (0113) 244 3168
for private hire + guest list

8 Harrison St
Leeds LS1 6P

word) doubles as a chill out area, but gets as packed as the main club. Never one to disappoint, Basics will be celebrating its ninth birthday this year so come enjoy the party with promoter and man about town Mr Dave Beer. 'Crasher kids are warned to keep well clear, the freak who turned up with a glow-stick and bonkers hair-do was suitably laughed out of the place. Only Mr Beer is allowed the wacky hair.

Planet Earth
City Square 243 4733
The bastion of revolving cheese. Mainstream dance is the staple of most nights here, but it's worth a visit to watch very pissed people trying to navigate th spinning dance floor with grace, and fai ing miserably. It doesn't pretend to b anything other than a pissed u night–spot, and for that it deserve drunken applause. STOP PRESS. Re opening as Bondi Beach Bar in Sprin 2001. Expect a little ray of Australian sur shine in Leeds - with a revolving danc floor.

Po Na Na
Assembly Street 243 3247
A souk bar no less. Soul, funk, drinkin and dancing. The interior is worth a mer tion, if only for the beautiful, hug lanterns adorning the walls. Palms an

Hand book

www.itchyleeds.co.uk

red velvet seem to be the way to go if you want to create a good atmosphere and promote a chill out vibe. Gets very busy at the weekends so get there early - it's usually free before 10. DJs play every permutation of house music known to man and a fair slab of funk and soul; and if that's not enough true entertainment comes in the form of sitting at the main bar counting and giggling at the hordes of people that walk straight into the massive mirror that looks like another room. Five points for a dropped drink, ten for a bloody nose.

Ritzys
Merrion Centre
Cheesy and sleazy. If you're not familiar with the get up and fall down philosophy of clubbing, maybe you need a lesson in Ritzy etiquette. Get up, put your make up and clothes on, drink cider, struggle to Ritzys, drink more cider, and fall down. There are, of course, the options to snog, fight or vomit, but these are strictly for the professionals. Sex is available, and probable…if you're not choosy.

The Space
Hirsts Yard 243 1030
The relatively new kid on the clubbing block, and currently taking Leeds by storm (expect to queue). This is the place to go if you've just been on a shopping spree in the big smoke and bought that vital Dispensary piece that's not yet stocked in Leeds. Your efforts will not go unnoticed daahhhling. The music is a diet of 100% house.

Think Tank
Call Lane
If you've got a floppy fringe and eyebrows that join in the middle there's not much left in Leeds for you, so this will be your oasis. Saturday plays host to the once legendary Automatic, churning out familiar anthems that draw the staggering Liam'n'Noel clones onto the floor, preaching the legendary lyrics to each other with a beer in one hand and a voddie in the other. Bring back any memories? If it doesn't, dig out the Stan Smiths and Fred Perry shirt, get down there, wait for them to play Fool's Gold and I bet you head straight for the floor and swagger with the best of 'em. Skanky-cool underground venue, that feels like a proper club.

RIZLA+ It's what you make of it.

Hey Baby, what's your Hotmail address?

Isn't it time to change your chat up line?
With MSN® Hotmail® whoever you pull can instantly go into your little black online book. What's more you can access your email any time, from any internet enabled PC – and your account is free. Don't miss out – visit *www.studenthotmail.co.uk* now and get your own personal email account.

email me ☐ @Hotmail

Microsoft
Where do you want to go today?®

Microsoft, the Microsoft logo, 'Where do you want to go today?', MSN,
the MSN butterfly device and Hotmail are either registered trademarks
or trademarks of Microsoft Corporation in the US and/or other countries.

msn Hotmail

Po Na Na

MONDAYS • PASSENGER 2000 • FREE BEFORE 10PM
AIRPORT TAX £3 MEMBERS / £4 NUS / £5 WITHOUT

TUESDAYS • EL RITMO LATINO • FREE BEFORE 10 PM
£3 10PM - 11PM / £4 AFTER (£1 NUS DISCOUNT)
SALSA LESSONS - INTERMEDIATE 7.30PM / BEGINNERS 8.30PM

WEDNESDAYS • FUNKTONE 5000 • FREE BEFORE 10PM
£4 (£3.50 CONCESSIONS) • SCRATCH DJS WITH LIVE MUSICIANS

THURSDAYS • FATMAN • FREE BEFORE 10PM
£2 AFTER • FAT FUNKY BREAKS

FRIDAYS • THE NORTHERN LINE • FREE BEFORE 10PM • £3 10PM - 11PM / £5 AFTER
FUNK / SOUL / HIP HOP / ACID JAZZ FROM BLUE NOTE LONDON

SATURDAYS • FUNKJUNXION / NEXTMEN / JOE 90 & SUSS / ZEN MASTERS
FREE BEFORE 9.30PM • £3 9.30PM - 10.30PM / £5 10.30PM - 11.30PM / £7 AFTER
BREAKBEAT / BIGBEAT / HIP HOP & CLASSIC UPTEMPO FUNK

SUNDAYS • AVAILABLE FOR PRIVATE HIRE

2 Assembly Street, Leeds   0113 243 3247
www.ponana.co.uk

Wardrobe

St Peters Building (next door to W. Yorks Playhouse)

If you ever catch them playing a load of very similar beats in short succession, you know they've failed in their quest to bring a more sophisticated, laid back club to the city. The ground floor is a classy late bar frequented by those who want a more relaxed, conversation-led night out, while downstairs, the club churns out jazz and latino, rather than the usual diet of pounding beats, gurning and telling everyone your name 87 times an hour.

SMS : INBOX

Basement Jaxx at
The Junction
on Mon 21st. See
www.itchyleeds.co.uk
for more details.

OPTIONS   BACK

Have news and events for your favourite music sent to your phone

RIZLA+   www.rizla.com

clubs

club listings

CLUB	Night	Music Genre	Cost	Misc
MON				
The Fav		Band Night-live music	Free	Bar dash
Evolution	Student Night	Chart Dance hits	£3 with NUS	All drinks reduced
Hi-Fi Club	Sweet Revival	R&B, Hip-hop, soul	£3.50- £3 NUS	Drink Promos
Po Na Na	Passenger 2000	Funk, hip-hop, garage	£4/£2 Members	Shooters £2, Carling £1.50
TUES				
Cockpit	Tuesday Session	Indie Midweeker	£3	
The Fav		Hip Hop and R&b	Free	Spirit doubles £1.50 allday
Majestyk	Agenda	Chart and dance	£1 NUS	Drink Promos
Po Na Na	The Latin Quarter	Salsa classes	£3, 9-11/ £4 aft	beginners 8.30, Interm 7.30
The Space	Chopper	House, D'n'B, Hip Hop	£3	£1, Tequila, Vodka.
WED				
The Atrium	Event Horizon	Dark drum 'n' bass	£5	Last of every month
Cockpit	Dust	Hip-Hop, Drum 'n' Bass	£3	
Cockpit	Skamageddon	Ska, Punk, Metal	£3.50	Last of every month
Elbow Room	East Village Café	Jazz, Groove, Funk	Free	Free Pool and cockail
Evolution	Logical Progression	Drum and Bass	£7/6	No hoods, hats, caps
The Fav		Cheesy choons		
Hi-Fi	Moveonup	N Soul, Motown	£3.50, £3 membs	Drink Promos
Majestyk	Boogie M	70's, 80's, 90's	£2/3.Free b4 11	
	Funksploitation	Funk, Hip-Hop, Beats	£1b4ll£2 after	Shooters £2
The Space	Base	Hard and Funky House	£4/5/6	Tequila, Vodka £1
THURS				
Cockpit	Poptastic	Pop and indie	£3.50	Gay friendly night
66 Boar Lane	The Grind	Garage and RnB	£3	Selected discounted drinks
The Fav	DJ Competition	Various	Free	Loadsa giveaways
Heaven	Damnation	70's, 80's, 90's	£3	£1 selected drrinks all night
Hell	Damnation	House, Garage, Trance	£3	£1 Selected drinks
Mint	Stush			
Po Na Na	I Love Lucy	Hip-Hop, Funk, Electro	£1 after ten	Carling £1.50
The Space	Funky Wormhole	Funk	£4/Free B4 11	
Think Tank	Mambo No7	Funky pop and dance	£3/£2 b4 11	Selected bottles £1.50
Warehouse	Tequila	Dance, Chart, Party	£4/5	£3 Members

Flick through the papers

www.itchyleeds.co.uk

FRI

66 Boar Lane	Elegance	Hard House/trance	£5	Discounted drinks
Atrium	Cooker	Funk, house, grooves	£6	In it's 8th year!
Cockpit	Hallelujah	Manchester sounds	£5adv/£6	First of the month
Cockpit	Brighton Beach	Indie, Mod	£5 adv	4th Friday of the month
Cockpit	Templehead	Techno	£8 adv	10pm-6am
Elbow Room	Friday Funktion	Eclectic funk &House	£4/£3 B4 11	Free weekend flyer, available
Evolution	Red	UK Garage	£4/£3	coach from city square every 15 mins
Fluid	Humjam	UK House and Garage	£6/5	Over 20's, no sportswear
The Fav	ID	experimental	£3/2 NUS	Reduced cocktails and beer
Fruit Cupboard	Frisco Disco	Funky Disco	£4/6	
Fuse	Housetrap	Garage grroves, house	£5/6	
Heaven & Hell	Redemption	70's 80's 90's	£6	Smart clobber, no trainers
Hi-Fi Club	FunkSoulNation	70's funk, rare grooves	£6/£5 NUS	
Majestyk	Wonderland	Commercial dance	£4/5	
Mint	Acces all Areas			
Po Na Na	The Northern Line	Big beat, hip-hop	free b4	
Think Tank	Come Together	Indie anthems, britpop	£5 /£4 b4 11,	Selected bottles £1.50
The Space	Union	Progressive House	£8/£7 concs	Global Underground
Warehouse	Sid Fox	Drum 'n' Bass	£6/7	
Wardrobe	Casa Latina	Hardcore salsa/reggae	£6/5	Real carnival feel

SAT

After Dark	The Orbit	Deep/Tech house		Drink promos
Atrium	Filling the Gap	Soulful deep house	£7/£5 b4 11,	Live music
Cockpit	The Garage	Indie, skate, alternative	£4 adv	
Evolution	House, Garage		£5	20+ No denim
Elbow Room	St Saturday	Old skool	£3 after 11	Food served all night
Fluid	Fundada	American vocal house	£9/8 NUS	Over 21's
The Fav	Homework	Lessons in House	£3/2 NUS	1st and 3rd of the month
The Fav	Flint plays........	Fresh, funky beats	£3/2NUS	4th of the month
Fruit Cupboard	Sugar Daddys	Funk, 80's soul, r'n'b	£7/£5 members	10pm-4am
Fuse	F**ed Up	Hard house all nighter	£9 /10 others	Open til 6am
Heaven & Hell	Salvation	70's, 80's and 90's	£6	Smart, no trainers
Heaven & Hell	Glasshouse	Bouncy uplifting house	£8/10 guests	2am-12noon
Majestyk	Magic	Funky House	£6	Over 20's
Mint	Basics	Deep, funky house	£8 /£10	James Holroyd
Po Na Na	Big Saturdays	Hip-hop, funk big beat	£3-7	Happy hour 'til 10pm
The Space	Stereo	Uplifting, vocal house	£8 /£10	Dress code applies
Think Tank	Automatic	Sleazy indie	£5/6	
Wardrobe	Yardbird Suite	Jazz and Groove	£7/6 members	
Warehouse	Speed Queen	Happy voccal house	£8 /£10	Best dressed club in England

For more up-to-date club reviews, previews and listings check:

www.itchyleeds.co.uk

RIZLA www.rizla.com

clubs

69

gay
www.itchycity.co.uk

Bars and Pubs

Queens Court
Lower Briggate 245 9449
The outside courtyard in this, Leeds' only 100% gay bar and club (and with a name like that what else could it be?), make it the perfect venue for a spot of talent watching whilst you chill out in the relaxed atmosphere. A club upstairs means you don't have to venture more than 30ft for an all-round good night.

The Bridge Inn
Bridge End 244 4734
As with many venues in Leeds this traditional pub is enjoying the relaxed drinking now available with the introduction of a 2am licence. A popular haunt for the locals.
Sunday – Throwback
Monday – Relaxation
Tuesday – Chart Attack
Wednesday – R'n'B night
Thursday – Karaoke with Judy
Friday/Saturday – Dance the night away with disco

The New Penny
Call Lane
Not the place to go if you want to show off that new shark fin hair-do, as this pub attracts an older crowd. Get yourself a leather outfit though, and you're talking. The sort of place a Londoner would expect of a northern gay pub, complete with the occasional stripper. Cabaret nights, karaoke and drag acts ensure that the main stay of its clientele are catered for throughout the week.

Blayds Bar
Lower Briggate 244 5590
That cashmere ensemble that you've been saving for a special occasion might not be such a good idea here as you're likely to snag it on the pine furniture. If you're looking for a quiet place to have an intimate chat then look no further – but not on a Wednesday. If you're a fan of opera you'll love it!

The Old Red Lion
York Road 273 5573
Further afield than its comrades, this huge pink pub (really!) tends to attract an older crowd. Perhaps it's something to do with the pool table, the only one in a gay pub in Leeds.

Velvet
Hirsts Yard 242 5079
Quite a mixed crowd, so if you don't mind rubbing shoulders with some up-for-it clubbers and the more relaxed end of Leeds' social spectrum, this is the place. Quieter during the week but a full on party at the weekends (pre-club venue to Speed Queen).

Fibre
Lower Briggate 08701 200 888
(see Bars)
New addition to the Leeds gay scene. Great place for chilling out, as it's fairly quiet during the week, leading to a more charged weekend atmosphere. Cool décor and mixed clientele.

Club Nights

Speed Queen@Warehouse
Speed Queen is an institution. The only place to go on a Saturday night for the clubber who wants to stay up way past their bedtime and dance 'til dawn. All forms of weird regalia are welcomed: in fact the weirder the better. It's like being at a really BIG party and the mixed crowd ensures an 'anything-goes' policy. Downstairs is pure hedonism with funky and uplifting house, whilst upstairs you can take a respite under the fans with a bit of R'n'B. Alternatively you can lounge on the beds with your new 'best friend'.

Poptastic Thursdays@Cockpit
Great for that 'weekend warm-up'. Poptastic is a fusion of indie and cheesy pop – oddly enough. Not one for those who prefer to look like they've just stepped out of a salon – it gets particularly sweaty, but surely that adds to all the fun?

From	Subject	Received
itchycity.co.uk	Gay news and events by e-mail	Thu 02/11/00 1...

shopping

www.itchycity.co.uk

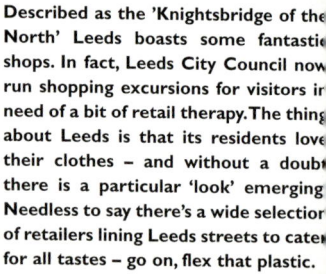

Described as the 'Knightsbridge of the North' Leeds boasts some fantastic shops. In fact, Leeds City Council now run shopping excursions for visitors in need of a bit of retail therapy. The thing about Leeds is that its residents love their clothes – and without a doubt there is a particular 'look' emerging. Needless to say there's a wide selection of retailers lining Leeds streets to cater for all tastes – go on, flex that plastic.

Shopping Areas

Granary Wharf
The Canal Basin (behind the city rail station, under the arches) 244 6570
If you're looking for an alternative to the high street stores that litter Leeds, then you might want to check out the new look Wharf. Housed under the railway arches, the intriguing enclaves offer a genuinely unique and specialist shopping haven. From Buon Appetito (speciality imported food from Italy) to Morgana

(alternative clothing: punk, goth, glam) you'll find the cool stuff that you never knew you were looking for until you see it. Spend leisurely Bank Holidays and weekends meandering about the array of stalls offering innovative one-offs, whilst being entertained by musicians and street artists. There's also some fabulous eateries, including the new Café Vitae, which is a recruitment consultants and café-bar all rolled into one. Good parking facilities. Open 10-6pm seven days.

Corn Exchange
Call Lane 234 0363
A wonderfully historic centre for retail therapy. Nestling within its curvaceous walls are loads of small independent shops, specialising in street-orientated styles, clubbing regalia, kitsch gifts and household items. There are also some

UNUSUAL GOODS AND GIFTS

GRANARY WHARF is a speciality shopping centre, with non-High-Street goods you **will not find** anywhere else. Open seven days, with additional market stalls every weekend.

Granary Wharf
LEEDS WATERFRONT

Located next to Leeds Rail Station, behind the Hilton Hotel.

www.granary-wharf.co.uk

great music stores selling up-front vinyl that you might have trouble getting hold of elsewhere. The Corn Exchange has recently undergone a massive refurb, introducing Elemental – a new café-bar situated in the basement, that offers an extensive daytime menu and is fully licensed. From Friday to Sunday the ground floor plays host to a kind of up-market craft fair showcasing all sorts of odd gift ideas. There's also the opportunity to see art displays from time to time providing a respite from the shopping frenzy that's going on around you.
Mon-Sat: 9-5.30pm, Sun: 10.30-5pm.

Victoria Quarter
Briggate 245 5333

In my opinion, the best place to shop if you're feeling flush. A victim of its own success in a sense, as it was originally supposed to house independent stores, but has now given way to upmarket national chains which take up nearly every unit. It does look great though, with its immaculate décor, street cafés and the beautiful people of Leeds lurking around. Extend that overdraft and enjoy.
Mon-Sat: 9-6pm, Sun: 11-5pm.

White Rose Centre
Dewsbury Rd (jnc 28, M62) 229 1234

Shopping mall; big covered arcade filled to the brim with chain stores like BHS and Debenhams. It would be great when it's raining but for the fact that it's filled with the usual dull chain stores, and it gets so busy that walking round the place is like some kind of Japanese endurance punishment. If you do get dragged there, the only saving grace is HMV and the fact it's nowhere near as big as places like Meadowhall and the Trafford Centre, so it means you don't have to stay there as long.   Best avoided between the months of January to December inclusive.
Mon-Fri: 10-10pm, Sat: 10-7pm, Sun: 11-5pm.

Unisex

Accent
Queens Arcade
Women 244 2414   Men 243 1707

Fine clothing for men, women and children, across three stores. Probably has the best denim selection in the city, which is good for those who find it a real nightmare fitting into your standard department store sizes. There's also some fabulous jewellery sold in the ladies store, made right here in Leeds, by a lovely lass named Emma Nosurak. Stocks Red or Dead, Diesel, Armani and Versus to name but a few. You've no excuse not to impress any more.

Ace
Duncan St 245 4555
Your disco needs you. So make an effort. If you're trying to cultivate that 'clubbing in lycra' style-look no further. Funky finds, along with kitsch household items. A shop to visit when you're trying to find a pressie for the person that has everything. (I've never met that person).

Envy
Briggate 245 8045
Sitting at the very top of Briggate, it's hard to forget about Envy, not necessarily for the quality of clothes but more the loud choons blaring out the door. Lots of labels including French Connection, Firetrap and Peter Werth plus very snazzy changing rooms.

Exit
Corn Exchange 246 9301
Kitting out Leeds' skate kids with Mambo, Paul Frank and plenty of baggy threads. More than enough for everyone who says 'dude' a lot.

Flannels

Vicar Lane 234 9977
This beautiful space houses a good selection of designer wear. One to check out if you like your expensive threads a little on the conservative side. The girls fare better with Jil Sander, Katherine Hamnett and Versus, with the odd shoe thrown in for good measure. One request? Can we have a few items in a colour other than black?

Harvey Nichols
Briggate 204 8888
Heaven for the label whore. All the obvious collections stocked as well as their

THE INDEPENDENT ON SUNDAY — The best writers, the sharpest opinions

own range. Large selection of accessories for men and women, a good food hall, and a bizarre selection of home furnishings. The accessories on offer are to die for, but my advice is to wait until sale time when they have magnificent reductions. Careful not to extend that lunch break too long in order try on all the fabulous Miu Miu, Prada and Gina shoes. You'll definitely need that promotion to fill the wardrobe

Hip
Thorntons Arcade
Men 242 4617
Ladies 234 7655

All you need for urban street style. Duffer, Stussy, Diesel and Evisu for the boys, Hysteric Glamour, Dispensary, YMC and associated sassy gear for the laydees. Always one step ahead in the style stakes. Two stores.

Morgan
Victoria Quarter 243 4616

You know what to expect from this high street chain store. It might come from France but that doesn't mean it's stylish. Walk in a funky chick, walk out a walking billboard. With all that free advertising via their name emblazoned tops they should be paying you to wear the clothes.
Own brand clothing now available for men too.

Strand
Briggate 243 8164

Stylish surroundings and stylish clothing for both guys and gals. Mandarina Duck, Chloe, Elvis and Jesus, D&G, Helmut Lang and Paul Smith all rub shoulders with the contemporary shoe and jewellery collections. Beautiful, stylish, perfection – don't go on an ugly day.

Uth
Vicar Lane 244 9464

Formerly Jigsaw for men, this good-looking store has metamorphosised into a contender for best unisex retailer in Leeds. The new name better reflects the young modern street style for tha' boys and sloaney get-up's for the girls, Uth has certainly filled a gap in the market. Have chains ever been this good?

d a w n   s t r e t t o n

*l a d i e s   d e s i g n e r
e v e n i n g w e a r*

Unit CB3, The Corn Exchange Shops,
Call Lane, Leeds, LS1 7BR. Tel: 0113 244 9083
e-mail: dawn.stretton@btclick.com

w w w . d a w n s t r e t t o n . c o m

Vivienne Westwood
Victoria Quarter 245 6403

Can't find that elusive pair of eighteen inch platform stiletto's? Look no further than Viv's joint. A jewel in the British fashion scenes' crown and the best looking clothes in Yorkshire by far.

Ladies

Dawn Stretton
Corn Exchange 244 9083
Luxury is having your clothes hand made, and this is certainly the order of the day at Dawn Stretton, which sells a selection of beautiful designs, in exquisite fabrics for all occasions.

Joseph
Vicar Lane 242 5450
There are now more 'Sloanies' in Leeds than Knightsbridge so this store does very well. You know what to expect, no where to tie up the horse though.

Galaxy 105 THE NEW MIX FOR YORKSHIRE

Karen Millen
Victoria Quarter 244 6505

Quality ladies clothing and now a fantastic selection of shoes. Wait for the sales when the clothes begin to get close to reasonably priced.

Plastique
Corn Exchange
Cool, if you like your clubwear on the garish side…

Retro Woman
Victoria Quarter 244 8230
Choose from Elise Ryan, Catwalk collection and Maggie Ray as well as other desirable individual items.

Speed Queen
King Charles St 246 1033
Can't find a pair of glittery eyelashes to match your boob tube? Fear not as Speed Queen's got it covered. Wigs, nails, glitter, diamante – a magnet for magpies. Small collection of clothes as well, from plastic knickers and metal dresses to more extravagant get ups.

Swan
Corn Exchange 245 4364
Own brand club and smart wear. The essential place to go for that one off item.

Vicky Martin
Victoria Quarter 244 1477
Chain mail and lycra specialists. Butt beware bloaters, the sizes are tiny. However they will be more than happy to do alterations.

Men

Aspecto
Victoria Quarter 245 0150
Shoes upstairs – Nike, Patrick Cox, Clarks, Camper, Birkenstock. Clothing for men downstairs – DKNY, Carhart, Phat Farm and cohorts.

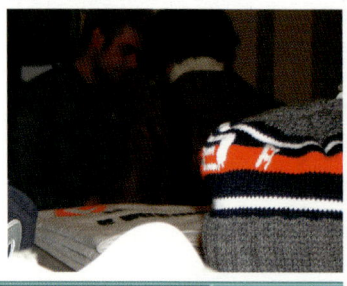

Address http://www.itchyleeds.co.uk Go

78

CORKER

RIZLA + WARE

For the full Rizlaware range just visit www.rizla.com or call 07000 749527

CHIMP

Stocking: Converse, Burro, Fly, Freshjive, Spiewak, Etnies etc

0113 234 9979

Chimp
Thorntons Arcade   234 9979
Chimp goes boldly where other clothing shops fear to tread. Selling a diverse range of left of centre merchandise; clothing from Burro, to objects of desire-check out the cool Converse range.

Life
Victoria Quarter   234 3971
Stone Island, Armani Jeans and Rockport. Don't forget the affected Mancunian accent – even if you're from Pontefract.

Primo
Victoria Quarter   234 3863
Hope and Glory, Peter Werth and the like from this straight down the middle store.

Record Shops

Bassspace
**(above Polar Bear) Grand Arcade
234 3354**
Good selection of up to the minute tunes with a house slant.

Big Deal
Vicar Lane   244 3882
Good secondhand instrument selection as well as synths and music systems.

Borders
Briggate   242 4400
As well as reading material, Borders houses a comprehensive CD section upstairs and stacks of listening posts. It's open late, but can be a bit pricey.

Crash Records
The Headrow   243 6743
A good selection of vinyl – house, jungle, drum and bass, R'n'B, hip hop as well as a comprehensive CD section upstairs.

Galaxy 105   THE NEW MIX FOR YORKSHIRE

Desperate Dan's
Back Kensington Terrace, Hyde Park
230 6119
Purveyors of second hand CDs and vinyl. Perfect for spending Sunday afternoon searching for elusive tunes.

Hellraiser
Call Lane
Rock dude! Tees too.

HMV
Victoria Walk 245 5548
If you can't find or order it here you've been imagining it.

Jumbo
St Johns Centre 245 5570
Worth the trek through the Bermuda triangle that is the St John's Centre. Stocking a mesmerising array of vinyl as well as CDs and tapes, Jumbo appeals to the collector as well as the browser.

Loop
Corn Exchange 242 0506
New to the Corn Exchange, on the second floor, with a grade A selection of vinyl and compilation tapes. This small but perfectly formed store also sells some great clothing. Friendly staff and listening posts to boot. There's gems in them there racks.

Mix 'N' Midi
Corn Exchange
246 8642
Check out those jockey sluts. All you'll ever need for making bedroom mix tapes.

---

loop
music & clothing

Specialists in

Progressive house/Hard house & Trance. Deep house. Funky/Disco house. Breaks & Beats/Downtempo. Funk/Disco

Also available at Loop Music & Clothing.

White labels/Bootlegs & Promos.

Official stockists of Oeuf clothing and other exclusive labels as worn by the stars.

Cheaper than most.

The Corn Exchange, Leeds
0113 242 0506

www.daloop.fsnet.co.uk
e:loopinleeds@mail.com

Out Of Step
Crown Street
245 1730
Punk, hardcore and hip hop to be found amongst skate clothes and boards.

Pat Brady's Soul Records
Mail order only 230 4342
Pay £2 a month and receive details of how to order Wigan classics you've been searching for.

shopping

FORBIDDEN (SCOTLAND) LTD. PLANET

For the best selection of
comics
toys
videos
models
t-shirts
science fiction
media books

Check out our massive range of
Star Trek
Buffy
Pokemon
Star Wars
Xena
Simpsons
Wrestling Merchandise

**30 Eastgate, The Headrow, Leeds LS2 7JL
0113 242 6325**

Play Music
Corn Exchange 234 1745
A new addition to the Leeds music scene fronted by a collection of 'faces about town'. Offering a variety of up-front vinyl from house to electro, techno to garage. Well-informed staff, cool décor and impromptu sets from the likes of Ralph Lawson demonstrate the superiority of this well-stocked deck twiddler's paradise.

Polar Bear
North Lane Headingley 230 7232
Grand Arcade 243 8231
Fantastic across the board second hand collection on CD, and excellent catalogue to find that far-out jazz re-issue.

Record Box
New Briggate 242 2488
All you vinyl junkies will be in heaven searching through the racks of second hand plastic on offer.

Relics
New Briggate 234 7361
Seen High Fidelity? You'll recognise the people in here.

Sound Control
Aireside Centre 242 6601
Big, just-out-of-town specialists for instruments (except brass and drums) and midi gear. Sells all manner of music systems too.

Sub Level Records
Hyde Park Corner 230 4585
Diversifying has led to a larger clientele over the last year. This record store stocks techno, house, hip-hop and trance as well as second hand stuff.

Trax
Corn Exchange 0780 115 1097
Try to buy your new CD's cheaper.

Virgin Megastore
Albion Street 243 8117
Videos, CD's, tapes and a small selection of vinyl as well as games and posters. Keep clear of the singles racks unless you want to get trampled by an eight year old on his/her way to grab Britney's latest release.

FIND THE NEAREST CASHPOINT ON YOUR WAP PHONE
wap.itchycity.co.uk

shopping

Games

Arcadia
51 New Briggate 293 0343
Second hand games for all you junkies.

Electronic Boutique
Albion Street 242 8957
Chain store offering the usual crop of games alongside a small second hand section.

Gamestation
Market Buildings 246 9353
New and used games brought to you from guys who know what they're talking about.

Gifts

Anne Summers
Lands Lane 242 2608
Need a pair of crotchless knickers for that first date? Look no further.

Argent
Thorntons Arcade 247 0055
Beautiful hand made jewellery alongside ceramics and glassware.

Azendi
Otley Rd, Headingley 278 6176
Out of town purveyors of all things gift orientated, from glasses to watches.

Atticus
Hyde Park Corner 230 2989
Groovy gifts for cool cats. Choose from snazzy lamps, holographic table mats through to the best cards in town.

Buzz
Corn Exchange
Huge selection of posters, ideal for shared accommodation, or covering damp/cracks/randomly stained walls. Less effort than painting anyway…

Cadeuax
Victoria Quarter 244 9447
Top end of the gift market

✦ THE INDEPENDENT The best writers, the sharpest opinions

www.itchyleeds.co.uk

Condom Shop
Corn Exchange 244 6532
I'm sure you can imagine. And stop sniggering.

Gadget Shop
Headrow Centre 245 0509
Always packed and it's easy to see why. All the gadgetry you could ever need plus more gifts than you could know what to do with.

O and O
Briggate (opposite Allders side entrance) 234 0773
A gem of a store tucked away just off the Headrow selling jewellery, hand-made cards and other things pressie orientated. A real 'occasion' shop.

Other Cool Shops

Borders
Briggate 242 4400
Books and the most comprehensive magazine section in Leeds. Pick up a Village Voice and wish your life away. Small Paper Chase concession for all those missed birthdays. Open until 11 at night.

Forbidden Planet
The Headrow 242 6325
Comics, videos, posters and smart toys for those who don't want to grow up.

Loft
Dock Street 2428478
Fill that £200,000 one bedroom apartment with some gorgeously designed furniture.

TOP FIVE...
Pull (not fussy)
1. **Majestyk**
2. **Ritzy**
3. **Heaven And Hell**
4. **Brannigans**
5. **Observatory**

Lillywhites
Headrow Centre 234 0846
Sporting heaven with a dedicated Nike store housed within its three floors.

Movie Boulevard
Cherry Tree Walk 242 2888
Videos, posters and DVDs.

scooterworks

0113 217 7755

italjet

PEUGEOT Scooters

GO-PED

**60/62 Burley Road
Leeds, LS3 1JX**
sales@scooterworks.co.uk

Robert Mason
70 North Street 242 2434
A beautiful venue housing some beautiful designer furniture. There are some other gorgeous interior details on offer but they don't come cheap. Mind you, no loft space is complete without something from here – so go on, treat yourself!

Scooter Works
60/62 Burley Rd 217 7755
Jamie Oliver's got one, Italians look damn cool on them, and lets face it, it's better than cycling.

Travelling Man
Corn Exchange 242 7227
Games, comics and posters galore

Waterstones
Albion Street 244 4588
Books galore, be it for pleasure or academia as well as a cool little café on the first floor.

Wisdom
Crown Street 244 9129
Skateboards and cool skate orientated clothes.

It's 1:30 am. Where can I get a drink... with trainers on?
What time does that restaurant stop serving tonight?
I'm skint. Are there any happy hours at the moment?
Are there any decent garage nights on tonight?
Where am I going to find a wig for that 70's do tomorrow?
All your questions answered
at www.itchyleeds.co.uk

a Grillade	11 E5	Petit Provence	12 E3	Stick or Twist	54 D1
a Tasca	24 D4	Pitcher and Piano	41 H3	Strand	76 F4
en's Bar	51 C5	Pizza Express	17 G3	Strawberry Fields	9 -
eodis	8 G6	Planet Earth	64 E5	Sub Level Records	83 G4
ibrary, The	57 -	Plastique	78 G4	Suntanning	104 -
ife	80 F3	Play Music	83 G4	Swan	78 -
illywhites	85 E3	Po Na Na	64 G4	Take Aways	106 -
ittle Tokyo	21 G3	Polar Bear	83 F2	Tampopo	21 D3
oft	85 H5	Pool Court at 42	9 H4	Tariq's	19 -
oop	81 G4	Pret A Manger	90 E4	Tattoo Artists	103 -
S One	37 D3	Primo	80 G4	Taxis	112 -
ucky Dragon	20 F2	Purple Door	96 D5	Teatro	9 G5
ucky's	107 -	Queen's Court	70 G4	Telecabs	112 -
Mai Thai	22 G4	Quid Pro Quo	42 D4	Temple Newsam	98 -
Majestyk	63 E5	Quincey's	11 -	Teppenyaki	22 F2
Maxis	20 -	Quo Vadis	52 D3	Tequila Tequila	44 F3
Megabyte	91 -	Rascasse	12 F6	TGI Fridays	11 -
Mezze	37 G4	Rat and Parrot	52 D3	Thackeray Medical Museum	98 -
Milo	37 G3	Record Box	83 E2	Thai Siam	22 G5
Mint Club	63 D2	Relics	83 -	The Company	110 -
Mix 'N' Midi	81 G4	Retro Woman	78 G4	Think Tank	65 G4
Moderno	39 G4	Revolution	42 G4	Townhouse	44 G3
Mojo	39 F2	Riley Snooker Hall	95 F2	Travelling Man	86 G4
Morgan	76 F3	Ritzy's	65 E2	Trax	83 G4
Mouse House	91 -	Robert Mason	86 F2	Tropical World	98 -
Movie Boulevard	85 G4	Roc Bar	43 E5	Ultimate Skin Tattoo	103 E2
Napoleon's Casino	95 -	Rocket	43 G5	Uth	76 F3
New Jumbo	20 G3	Royal Armouries	98 -	Velvet	71, 27, 45
New Penny, The	70 -	Royal Park	56 -	Vicky Martin	78 -
No 36	39 D5	Sala Thai	22 -	Victoria Commercial Hotel	54 D3
Norman	39 G4	Salvo's	18 -	Victoria Quarter	74 F3
North Bar	40 F2	Scarborough Taps	53 F5	Virgin Megastore	83 E4
Northern Snooker Cnte	94,51 -	Scooter Works	86 -	Vivienne Westwood	77 G4
Observatory, The	51 F5	Shabab	19 E3	Walkabout	54 D2
Odeon, The	93 F2	Shear's Yard	9 G5	Wardrobe	46, 67 I2
Old Monk	52 E4	Shogun Teppenyaki	21 F6	Warner Brothers	93 -
Old Red Lion, The	71 -	Showcase	93 -	Waterstones	86 G3
Old Royal Oak	52 -	Sinbin	53 F3	Wellington, The	54 D5
Oporto	27, 40 G4	Skyrack	57 -	West Yorkshire Playhouse	93 H2
Original Oak, The	56 -	Slips Deli	90 -	Westgate Casino	95 -
Oscars	52 -	Soul Kitchen	43 D5	Whip, The	55 G4
Oslo	40 G4	Sound Control	83 G4	White Rose Centre	74 -
Out of Step	81 -	Sous Le Nez En Ville	12 E5	Whitelocks	55 F3
Pack Horse	57 -	Space, The	65 F4	Wisdom	86 G4
Paintball Commando	97 -	Speed Queen	78 D3	Yates's Wine Lodge	55 F4
Panninis	90 -	Spirit of St. Louis	10 F4	Yorkshire Dance	95 -
Parisa	41 E4	Springbok	53 E2	Yorkshire Paintball Centre	97 -
Pasta Romagna	17 F4	Square on the Lane	53 F4	Zest	91 D4
Pat Brady's Soul Records	81 -	Starbucks	90 -		

index

(Ca) Faluka	88	-
28 28	20	G2
Accent	74	G3
Ace	75	F4
After Dark	58	-
Aire	48	H4
Al Bacio	13	E3
AMF Bowling	96	D1
Amigos	24	H3
Andronicas	91	E3
Anne Summers	84	F3
Arcadia	84	F3
Argent	84	-
Artemis	25	-
Arts	24	G4
Ask	13	D4
Atrium, The	58	F2
Atticus	84	-
Azendi	84	-
Bagel Factory	90	F3
Bankers Draft, The	48	D3
Barcelona	60	-
Bassspace	80	F3
Beauty Salons	104	-
Bibi's	13	D4
Big Deal	80	G3
Big Lil's Saloon Bar	49	F2
Big Mama's	106	-
Bistro Fiori	15	F4
Blayds Bar	71	-
Borders	80, 85	F3
Boston Exchange	10	-
Box Creative Hairdressing	101	G4
Brannigans	49	F2
Brasserie 44	25	H4
Bridge Inn, The	70	H4
Brownes	49	C3
Buzz	84	G4
Cactus Lounge	23	H2
Cadeuax	84	F3
Café Vitae	89	F6
Caffe Uno	15	F3
Caliente Café	23	-
Calls Grill	7	H4
Canton Flavour	19	D3
Carpe Diem	49	D3
Chemic Tavern, The	55	-
Chimp	80	E3
Citrus	88	-
Citrus Pool Bar	94	-
City Cyber	91	D2
City Library	91	-
City Varieties	93	E3
Civic Theatre	93	C2
Clock Café	88	-
Club 66	60	F4
Cockpit	60	G5
Condom Shop	85	G4
Conservatory, The	49	E4
Corn Exchange	73	G4
Cottage Road Cinema	92	-
Crash Records	80	E3
Crusty Bin	89	-
Cuban Heels	23	H3
Da Mario's	15	-
Darbar	18	F4
Dare Café	89	-
Dawn Stretton	77	G4
Desperate Dan's	81	-
Digby's	60	C4
Dimitris	25	H5
Dino's	16	F6
Dolce Vita	15	F2
Dry Dock	57	-
Duck and Drake	50	H3
DV8	96	G4
Edwards	50	E2
Elbow Room	94	G5
Electronics Boutique	84	E4
Elephant Garden	18	G2
Empire Bar	50	D3
Envy	75	E3
Est Est Est	16	D4
Evolution	61	-
Exit	75	G4
Expo Hair	102	G4
F1 Racing	97	-
Fav, The	61	-
Felon and Firkin	50	C3
Fenton, The	57	-
Ferret Hall Bistro	6	-
Fibre	71	F4
Flannels	75	G3
Fluid	61	H3
Flying Pizza	16	-
Forbidden Planet	85	E3
Fortune Cookie	109	-
Frankie and Benny's	10	-
Freedom Divers	97	-
French Revolution	90	F3
Fresse Muncho	90	G3
Fruit Cupboard	61	G4
Fudge	36	H3
Fuji Hiro	20	E4
Fuse	62	G2
Gadget Shop	85	E3
Gamestation	84	G3
Golden Lion Hotel, The	114	G4
Granary Wharf	72	F6
Grand Theatre	93	F2
Grosvenor	95	D
Grove Café	89	-
Grove, The	50	-
Guildford, The	50	D3
Hairdressers	101	-
Hakuna Matata	36	G4
Hansa Gujarati	24	F2
Harewood House	97	-
Harry Ramsden	8	-
Harvey Nichols	75	F3
Harvey Nichols 4th Floor	8	F3
Headingley Taps	56	-
Health Clubs	100	-
Heaven and Hell	62	F2
Hellraiser	81	G5
Henry's	37	D3
Hi-Fi Club, The	63	F4
Hip	76	G4
HMV	81	F3
Hogshead	51	G4
Hollywood Bowl	96	-
Hyde Park	55	-
Hyde Park Picture House	92	-
Italian Job, The	17	G5
Jo and O	85	F3
Joseph	77	G3
Jumbo	81	E2
Kadas Coffee Lounge	89	G3
Karen Millen	78	F3
Kart Skill	97	-
Kirkstall Abbey	98	-
LA Bowl	96	-
La Comida	24	F5

E F G H

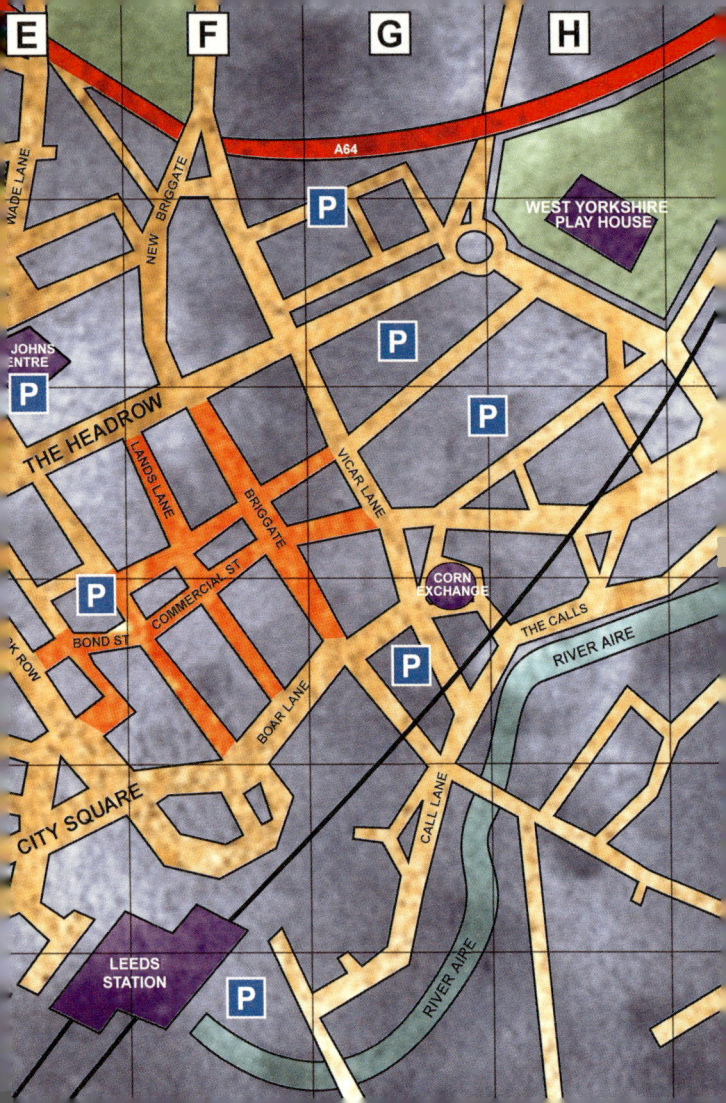

A64

WADE LANE
NEW BRIGGATE
JOHNS CENTRE
THE HEADROW
LANDS LANE
BRIGGATE
COMMERCIAL ST
BOND ST
ROW
VICAR LANE
WEST YORKSHIRE PLAY HOUSE
CORN EXCHANGE
THE CALLS
RIVER AIRE
BOAR LANE
CITY SQUARE
CALL LANE
RIVER AIRE
LEEDS STATION

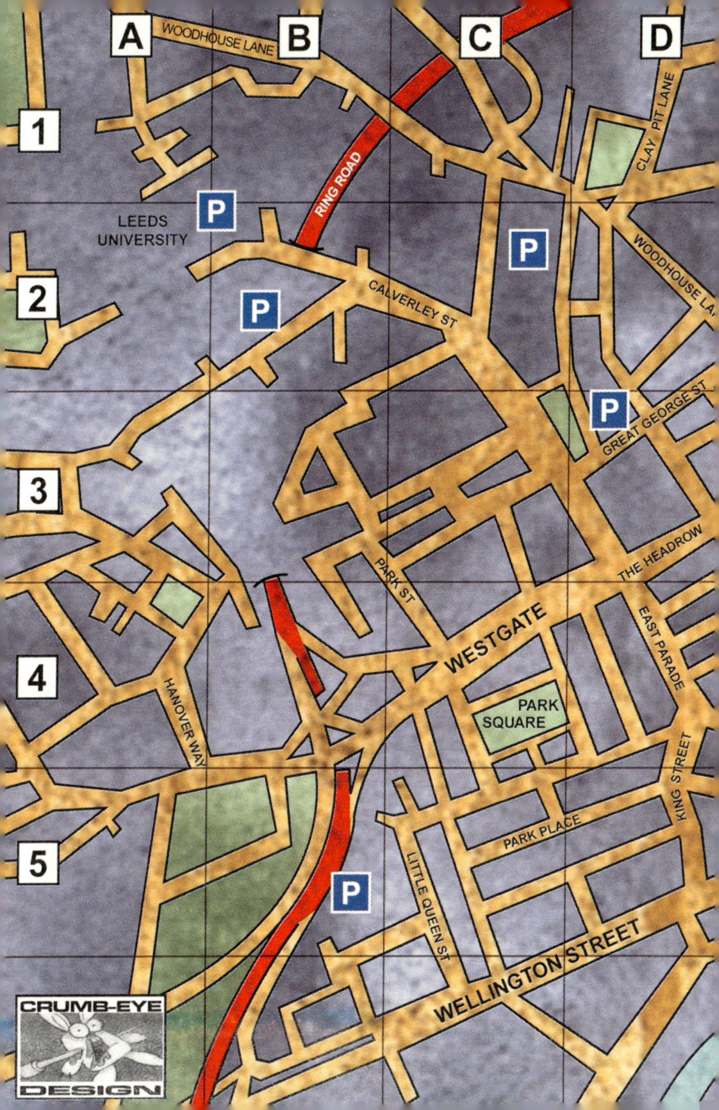

A
B
C
D
1
2
3
4
5
WOODHOUSE LANE
RING ROAD
CLAY PIT LANE
LEEDS UNIVERSITY
P
CALVERLEY ST
WOODHOUSE LA
GREAT GEORGE ST
THE HEADROW
PARK ST
WESTGATE
EAST PARADE
HANOVER WAY
PARK SQUARE
KING STREET
PARK PLACE
LITTLE QUEEN ST
WELLINGTON STREET
CRUMB-EYE DESIGN

50% off

GNER SuperAdvance return fares with a Young Persons Railcard and the same for a friend.

Here's something not to be missed. If you're a Young Persons Railcard holder, you can travel anywhere on the GNER route off-peak from 9 October 2000 to 5 February 2001 with 50% off our normal SuperAdvance return fares. A friend can travel with you for the same price, too. With a choice of 33 destinations to visit, there's no better way to see it, do it, and with the money you can save, buy the T-shirt.

Book now on **08457 46 46 37**
or at any GNER, selected ScotRail or Northern Spirit station.

www.gner.co.uk

Tickets are subject to availability. Please allow 3 working days for postage. Book at the latest before 1800 on the day before travel. Some travel restrictions apply.

Young Persons RAILCARD

GNER

T-shirt graphic:

youtwo
on tour
9 OCT 2000 - 5 FEB 2001
INVERNESS ◆ STIRLING ◆ GLASGOW
EDINBURGH ◆ BERWICK ◆ NEWCASTLE
YORK ◆ LEEDS ◆ HULL
DONCASTER ◆ GRANTHAM
PETERBOROUGH ◆ LONDON

Travel Inn
City Gate, Wellington St, (joined to TGI Fridays) 242 8104
£44.95 (+£5.25 for breakfast)

Budget

Budapest Hotel
12-14 Cardigan Rd, Headingley
275 6637
£29 week day, £26 weekend

Central Hotel
47 New Briggate 294 1456
£28

Clock Hotel
317-319 Roundhay Rd 249 0304
£25, £20 weekend

Cresent Hotel
274 Dewsbury Rd, Near Elland Road
270 1819
£19

Manxdene Hotel
154 Woodsley Rd, Hyde Park (near uni)
243 2586
£19

Hotel Booking Agencies

Expotel
Leeds Bridge House, Hunslet Road
Leeds. 242 3434

Tourist Info. Centre

Leeds Train Station 0113 242 5242

THE GOLDEN LION HOTEL

Special Rates For Clubbers.
Fridays & Saturdays.
3 Star City Centre Hotel.

From Only £27.50 pp/night

Lower Briggate, Leeds 0113 243 6454

www.itchyleeds.co.uk

Trains

National Rail Enquiries	0345 484950
Metro (train & bus)	2457676
GNER	0345 225225
Virgin Trains	0345 222333
Midland Mainline	0345 221125

Planes

Leeds Bradford Airport	2509696
Manchester Airport	0161 4898015

Car Hire

National Car Rental	2777997
Hertz	2429548
Budget	0800181181

Accommodation

Price for one night, single room with breakfast.

Expensive

42 The Calls
42 The Calls, City 244 0099
£98 weekday, £42.50 weekend

Hilton National Leeds
Neville Street, Near to rail, City
244 2000
£140 week day, £60 weekend

Malmaison
Sovereign Quay 398 1000
£105 week day, £75 weekend
Does not include breakfast

The Marriot
Boar Lane, City 236 6366
£127 week day, £72 weekend

Queens Hotel
City Square, City 243 1323
£115 week day, £45 weekend

Mid Priced

Golden Lion
Lower Briggate 243 6454
£99 week day, £50 weekend

Holiday Inn Express
242 6200
£62.50 week day, £55.00 weekend

Telecabs Taxis 0113 231 9000
www.telecabs.co.uk

getting about

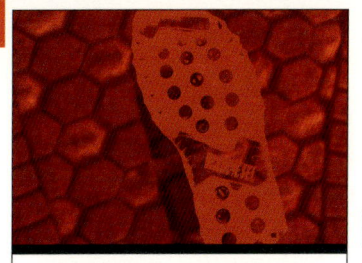

getting about, accommodation & map

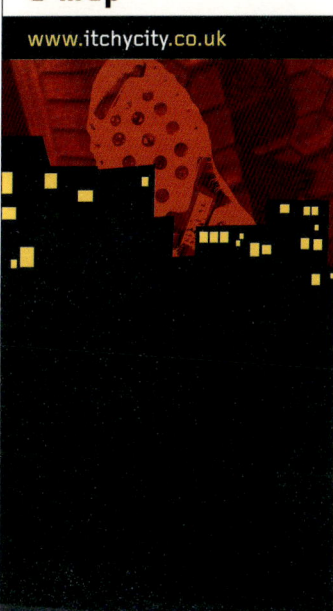

www.itchycity.co.uk

Taxi

Telecabs	2636666
	2792222
City Cabs	2469999
Streamline	2443322

Private Hire

Headingley Cars	2434445
Quickline	2444444
Ace Cars	2300060
Amber Cars	2306090
Blue Line	2445566
Furlongs	2267000
Parkways	2744441
Royal Cars	2305000
Top Line	2741000
Wheels	2499999

Buses

National Express	0990 808080
Yorkshire Coastliner	2448976
(Services to York and East Coast)	
First Leeds (local)	2420922
Black Prince (local)	2526033

www.itchyleeds.co.uk

GET THE CRAP OUT OF YOUR EARS

Galaxy 105

THE NEW MIX FOR YORKSHIRE

www.galaxy105.co.uk

Alcohol

The Company... with No Name.
0115 911 8000

The pubs are shut and the fridge is empty, but you still want to party. Nightmare! Not anymore though, as it's 'The Company.... with no name' to the rescue. Wines, spirits and beers delivered to your door until 4am. In fact they can supply everything you need for the complete party including BBQ and tent hire, and everything is completely legal and above-board, unlike some shady operations. Order between 5pm and 3.30am and expect delivery in approximately 30 minutes. Minimum orders apply.

Tel: 0115 911 8000

Chinese

Canton Flavour
Street Lane, Roundhay   269 6968

Fortune Cookie
Raglan Road, Hyde Park   244 2228
Free Phone 08000 155 444

Sakura
21 North Lane Headingley
224 2323

Jade House
3 Norwood Rd, Headingley
278 4537

Silver Vase
Stainbeck Lane   268 7033

Fish and Chips

Brett's Fish Restaurant
12-14 North Lane, Headingley
289 9322

Bryans of Headingley
9 Weetwood Lane, Headingley
278 5679

Chicken

Dixy Fried Chicken
New Briggate   246 9786

KFC
Arndale Centre, Headingley
275 5117

Free Delivery within a limited delivery area, min. order applies

Hao Yuns Fortune Cookie

Raglan Road, Hyde Park, Leeds
0113 244 2228
Open 7 days from 5pm 'til late

Freephone 08000 155 444

CHINESE Cuisine TAKE AWAY

Big Mama's

2744899
Open: Mon-Sat 'til 4 a.m

Booze Delivered
(4 Mile Area)
25 North Lane · Headingley

Kashmir
109 Chapletown Rd 262 5036

Moonlight Paan House
125 Brudenell Rd, Hyde Park.
230 7635

Nafees
68a Raglan Rd, Woodhouse. 245 3182

Nazam's
201 Woodhouse St, Kirkstall. 243 8515

Rajput Kebab House
3-4 St. Chad's Parade, Headingley
278 9008

Sultans
39 New Briggate, LS1. 293 0680

Luckys

To the untrained eye this may seem like a blatant plug, but the experienced Luckys diner will know what I'm talking about: Quite simply the pizzas are bloody good. It seems a bit of a waste that a lot of their business is done with pissed-up students, as to be honest, their top-drawer grub is wasted on them. Order some food before you've had 12 pints and you'll be shocked how good it is. They'll deliver it free, they do decent curries and if that weren't enough they've started a Chinese next door, to supply the residents of Headingley and Hyde Park with some quality noodles to boot. Yes, we know they're advertising, but if you don't like the grub, take this book back to where you bought it and demand your money back claiming we're damn liars. I bet you don't.

PIZZAS BURGERS DONERS CURRIES
LUCKYS

FreeFone 0500 11 33 45
FREE DELIVERY

Open 7 days 5pm 'til late

81 Raglan Road
Hyde Park
Leeds LS2 9DZ

LUXURY ORGANIC ICE CREAM

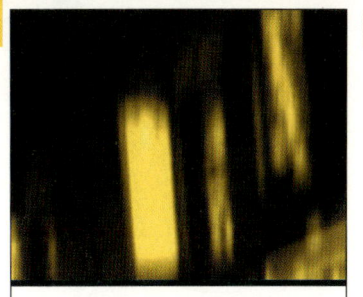

Pizza and Burgers

Big Mama's
25 North Lane, Headingley. 274 4899

Caesars Pizza
61 Brudenell Grove , Headingley.
278 0202

Café Pizza
68 Abbey Rd, LS5. 275 0000

Capone's Pizza
55 New Briggate, LS1. 242 5519

Dial-A-Pizza
3 Stanmore Hill, LS4. 278 5479

Dominos Pizza
88 Street Lane, LS8. 266 4488

Harpo's
Otley Rd, Headingley. 278 2415

Luckys
81 Raglan Rd. 0500 113345

McDonald's
St. Johns Centre. 242 0353
Briggate. 243 5548

Italiano's
111 Chapeltown Rd. 2392939
24 hour delivery

Indian

Massallas Indian Cuisine
275 Otley Rd, Headingley
230 2222

carrots aren't blue...

and shares aren't free

But we'll give you 1000 free shares in BlueCarrots when you join the growing community of BlueCarrots members who enjoy CashBack from a huge range of famous online stores. No catches, just CashBack.

BOL 7% CashBack	Mad About Wine 5% CashBack
Electrical Warehouse 6% CashBack	Magazine Shop 5% CashBack
Firebox 6% CashBack	Think Natural 5% CashBack
Games and Videos 5% CashBack	Kitbag 4% CashBack
Into Fashion 5% CashBack	Charles Tyrwhitt 5% CashBack

BlueCarrots.com
CashBack EVERY TIME you shop

shopSAFE

Name and occupation?
Wayne, Mobile phone salesman
Where do you bore people about tariffs? Fudge
And where do you dance to your novelty ringtones? Basics
You've made the sale, you've got a date. Where? Oslo
Where do you spend your commission? Play Music

Beauty

Handstanned
Grand Arcade 246 0030
Nail extensions, sculptured nails, tip and acrylic overlays, manicures. Enough pampering.
Mon 12pm-5pm, Tues 10am-5pm, Wed 10am-6pm, Thurs 10am-8pm, Fri 10am-7pm, Sat 10am-5pm.

One
Victoria Quarter 234 9600
Massages, spa treatments and tanning in the newest vanity spot in the Victoria Quarter.
Open 7 days, Mon-Fri 'til 8pm.

Roberto Mouras Hair and Beauty
22 Park Row 243 6842
Feel truly pampered in this beautiful salon, slap bang in Leeds financial district

Space NK
63 Vicar Lane (edge of Victoria Quarter) 242 6606
Immaculate shop/assistants and posh, rather expensive make-up.

Suntanning

Sun Quest
Call Lane 244 4441
By far the cheapest place to go for a false one. £1 for three minutes
Mon-Sat 8am-10pm, Sun 10am-10pm.

The Tanning Shop
New Station Street (near Yates on Boar Lane) 245 4560
Quick drop-in, stand-up tanning place in the city centre, £1 per minute
Mon-Fri 10am-7pm, Sat 10am-6pm.

Galaxy 105 THE NEW MIX FOR YORKSHIRE

Tattoo

Kaleidoscope (formerly Babs)
Church Walk 244 5504
For those girlies too scared to show their intimacies to a bloke.

Leeds Piercing Studio
Call Lane 242 0413
Not for the wallflower- and that's just the music. Belly button - £20
Mon- Fri 10.30-5, Sun 12-4

Pagan Body Piercing
Call Lane 242 4840
A calming experience. Belly £20
Mon- Sat 10-5, Sun 12-4

Steel Dreams
Hyde Park Corner
225 0405
Highly recommended, if you fancy a steel ring being put through a random part of your body.
Nipple-£25
Tues- Sat 1-6

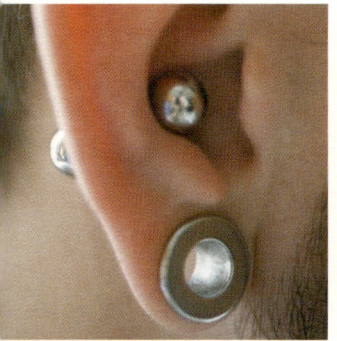

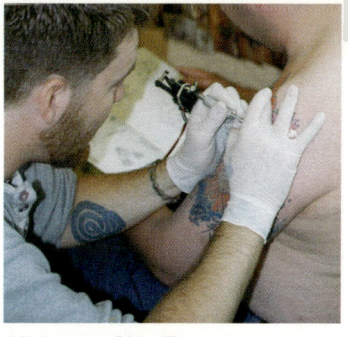

Ultimate Skin Tattoo
New Briggate
244 4940
The place to go for custom work and larger pieces. APTA member.
Open Tues-Sat: 12pm-8pm.

29A New Briggate
LEEDS UK LS2 8JD
+44 (0)113 244 4940
www.ultimateskintattoo.com

Expo Hair
White Cloth Hall, Crown St 234 7235
Situated next to the Corn Exchange, Expo is a well-established, well-respected hair salon. Students receive a 15% discount every day of the week and you can get a bargain haircut on Monday nights when training is in full swing. A huge range of services are on offer: real hair and monofibre extensions are available, handy for those trying to grow their hair, but can't face the inevitable mullet period (price on consultation - from £2 per extension), through to fashionable cuts for both men and women.
Women from £26.00, Men £24.00
Tues, Thurs, Sat 9-5, Wed 9-6, Thurs 9-8

Jam
Otley Road 278 6275
Far out far away little salon with bags of character.
Women and Gents from £18.00
Mon-Sat 9-6 (late night 8 occasionally - call for details)

Modern Hairdressing
Thorntons Arcade 245 4689
Well loved hairdressers for both sexes.
Lasses from £25.00, Fellas from £15.00
Mon/Tues/Wed 9-6, Thurs 9-8, Fri 9-6.30, Sat 8.30-5

Mega City One
Woodhouse Lane 242 3861
Sharp cuts and cutting edge treatments, ideally placed (and priced) for job-dodgers.
Women £15, Men £13
Tues- Sat 10- 5.15

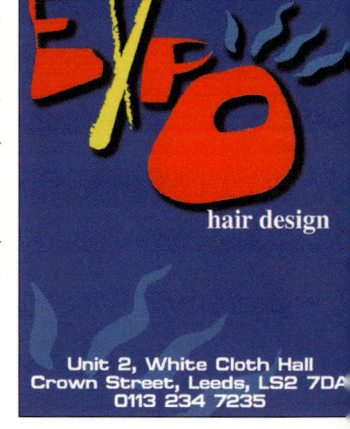

Oasis
Otley Road, Headingley 278 9214
Student specialities, although a total mix of people frequent this salon.
Women from £18.00 Men from £11.00
15% NUS Discount
Mon, Tues, Wed, Fri, Sat 9-6, Thurs 9-7

Toni and Guy
Boar Lane 234 4334
Cutting edge cutters.
Women £30.00, Men £24.00
Mon- Wed, Sat 9-5.30, Thurs Fri 9-6.15

EXPO hair design
Unit 2, White Cloth Hall
Crown Street, Leeds, LS2 7DA
0113 234 7235

one roof are three swimming pools, spa, sauna and steam room as well as a comprehensively equipped gym with over 100 pieces of equipment. It's just a matter of whether you can tear yourself away from the pub/TV…

Mon-Fri: 6am-12am, Sat/Sun: 8am-9pm. Monthly fees – £34 off peak, £42 all other times.

Hairdressers

Box Creative Hairdressing
Briggate 245 6869
Mon-Sat 10-6

This place has quite an enviable reputation. If you're already a regular you will have spent a fine half hour relaxing in the contemporary and stylish surroundings whilst hearing Craig's tales of Leeds' nightlife- it's a good place to pick up the latest bar news! Check out the traditional and avant-garde 'do's' on offer too. A haircut for the ladies will set you back £25.50, whilst 'something for the weekend' for blokes costs around £15.50. A full range of professional salon treatments and services are also on offer with colour treatments and more outlandish cuts.

BOX CREATIVE HAIRDRESSING
№3 LOWER BRIGGATE
LEEDS
0113 245 6869

City Gent
Otley Road, Headingley 230 6152
Mon – Sat 8.30-6
Boar Lane 244 4208
Mon- Sat 7.45- 6.30

Want a 'Beckham' but don't want to pay through the nose? This is the place. As you may have guessed they don't cater for the missis.
Prices start from £8.20

THE INDEPENDENT | The best coverage of news & sport

body

www.itchycity.co.uk

If, after all that shopping, you've worn yourself down, you could do worse than stagger down to one of Leeds' many fitness centres. Alternatively, sit back relax and let one of the qualified torturers (or tattooist and piercers a they are more commonly known) go to work on your most intimate areas.

Health Clubs

David Lloyd Leisure Leeds
Tongue Lane, Moortown
203 4000
When you wake, hacking up 50 Marlboro from the night before you know it's time to get to the pub, but you could do worse with... one of the largest gyms in Europe – indoor and outdoor pools, tennis, squash etc.
Open Mon-Fri: 6.30am-11pm, Sat/Sun 7am-11pm.
Membership from £42.50 (NUS)-£70.

Living Well
Hilton National Hotel
Neville St 244 5443
Tone yourself up with gym, sauna, swimming pool and whirlpool, then pig out in one of the hotels' many rooms.
Mon-Fri 6.30-10, Sat- Sun 7.30-8.
Membership £42 month, (£30 off peak 8-5 weekdays) plus joining fee.

Virgin Active
Cardigan Fields, Kirkstall Road
0845 301 2306
The mother of all health and fitness centres, this futuristic venture caters for all your fat bustin' needs. Included under

Two hours in Leeds

What, only two hours? Heaven only knows why you're not stopping longer, but if that's what you've got then in a whistlestop tour, you can...

- Run to the shops. For sheer flashiness, try the **Victoria Quarter** and **Harvey Nichols**, where you can drop in and admire the prices of cappuccinos in the **Express bar**.
- Fleece some random at the **Elbow Room**, have a vodka in **Norman**.
- Sprint into one of the many art galleries. **Leeds Art Gallery** is the most obvious choice with a diverse range of works.

A weekend in Leeds

This is more like it. Depending on your budget, you can recline in luxury at the **Queens Hotel**, sleep soundly for less than £30 at **The Golden Lion**, a comfy 3 star, or for pure comedy value (of the skanky cheap kind), get to the **Central Hotel**. They still have a wall of fame, with pics of Linda Lusardi and Chas & Dave.

Shopping

The choice is frightening. As per two hours, you're bound to stumble into **Harvey Nichols**, but for more affordable, funky independent stores, you might want to browse through the **Arcades**. For more vintage togs, try the **Corn Exchange**, where you'll find that kitsch pair of lilac flares you've been hunting for the best part of your life.

Daytime

If your Visa's knackered take a peek at **The Royal Armouries**, the only decent museum in the city, or get out to **Ilkley** (20 minute drive) and suck in some inspiration out on the **Moors**.

Eating

If you're trying to make an impression, give **Leodis** or **Rascasse** a whirl. Both will hurt your wallet, but worth it for something out of the ordinary. More affordable is **Arts Café**, with stunning local artwork and equally stunning food. If you're scraping the pennies together, go for **Fuji Hiro** for some good-value Japanese grub. Or – if you can be bothered to trek to Headingley – **Crusty Bins** for the best breakfast £3 can buy.

Drinking

Oporto for cool tunes. **Velvet** for cool people. **Mojo** for cool drinks. **The Square** for none of the above. Basically, head down to the Exchange Quarter by the Corn Exchange and get bar-hopping. There's not much in the way of dress codes (big groups of lads, forget it), but remember to look 'flamboyant' if you want to get in to **Oslo**. If all this high-class noncery gets on your nerves, try **Whitelocks** for a true Yorkshire pint.

Dancing

Leeds is famous for its ear bleed techno at **Orbit** on Saturday as well as the more sophisticated but equally messy **Basics** at **Mint**. For more pissed-up pulling revelry it has to be the infamous **Majestyk** or **Heaven and Hell** and for a more refined boogie it has to be **The Wardrobe**.

entertainment

Kirkstall Abbey
Kirkstall Road
Beautiful ruins of the old Abbey set in an acre of greenery with a river running beside it. Perfect for lazy days. During the summer it's possible to catch operatic performances in the early evening. Check itchyleeds.co.uk for details. There's also a small museum next door complete with a replica Victorian Street. Cor blimey guv'ner.

Name and occupation?
Sian, Student midwife
Favourite medicine cabinet?
Dry Dock
Puh, students. Student clubs your thing too?
Not at all. Queen's Court
What about food?
Roots & Fruits is my favourite
When you're not working 90-hour shifts, where you do shop?
Borders

Royal Armouries
Armouries Drive (Surprisingly)
0990 106666
Mon- Fri 10.30-5.30
Sat- Sun 10.30-4.30

If you've a penchant for guns and their associated paraphernalia you'll be in John Wayne heaven here. Firearms are documented historically in over 8000 exhibitions as well as live action shootouts and explosions. A thoroughly great day out. Adults £4.90. Concessions £3.90.

Temple Newsam
Off Selby Road 264 7321
Stately home of the Tudor/Jacobean order set in its own grounds of over 1000 acres. It's actually cited in the Doomsday book and houses many fine pieces of furniture and art.

Thackray Medical Museum
Beckett St 245 7084
10-5.30
£4.45, £3.60 concessions
Museum dedicated to hospitals, operations and the like, housed in a spectacular building near St. James hospital on the fringe of the city centre.

Tropical World
Prices Avenue, Roundhay Park
266 1850
10 'til dusk
£1.00, 50p concessions
Butterflies everywhere! Once you've got over that check out the massive ants going about their business alongside some ferocious looking plants, but spare a thought for the gorgeous and very intelligent marmosets looking a little on the depressed side. Monkeys, bats and some very cool fish. When there, find out more by grabbing a clipboard off any one of the school kids running around.

www.itchyleeds.co.uk

Karting and Paintball

F1 Racing
Monks Cross, York 0800 975 0853
'... And there goes Schumacher through the chicane...' Yes. It's in York, so try and leave the handbreak turns 'til you get here. That A64's one big speed trap.
£6 for 15 laps, £12.50 for 40 laps. Suzuka: 10 lap practice run with a 20 lap race, £15 per person for five people or more or £17.50 for groups of four and under.

Kart Skill
Riverside Raceway, Hunslet 249 1000
More fun than you can shake a gear stick at and in the heart of Leeds.
Tuition and race offer £10 per driver, for 30 laps with an average track time of 15 minutes. Subject to track availability, so give them a call beforehand.

Paintball Commando
Wakefield 01924 252 123
Paul in Human Resources giving you a hard time? Bring him here and kick the proverbial out of him.
Costs £15 per person including BBQ lunch and some free paint. Also a military style special forces 'it's a knockout type' affair, £40 per person with BBQ lunch.

Yorkshire Paintball Centre
Selby 01757 289 322
More messy and painful fun.
Costs £15 per person including 100 shots of paint and lunch.

PAINTBALL COMMANDO LEEDS

10 minutes from city centre
Paintball Games
Team Building Days
Special Forces Day
Junior Commando
birthday parties
day/half day/evening & party time events
Corporate Events

01924 252123

free refreshments & BBQ

Water Sports

Freedom Divers
380 Kirkstall Road 368 2828
Learn PADI for your hols. Diving trips and tuition

Days Out

Harewood House
Harewood 288 6331
Good family day out with entertainment for everyone, from extensive gardens, birds galore and fabulous views. What a lavahly hise sir.
£7.25 for adults, concessions £5.

From	Subject	Received
itchycity.co.uk	Theatre reviews and previews by e-mail	Thu 02/11/00 1...

Strip Joints

DV8
Lower Briggate   243 4293
Mon-Sat 'til 2am
Don't be fooled by the 'Tapas Bar' sign outside - you won't be eating in here, except for the carpet if you touch the merchandise, know what I mean?

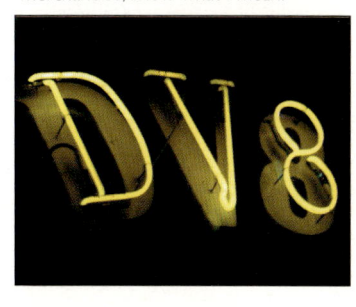

Purple Door
York Place   245 0536
Mon-Wed 5-2, Thurs-Fri 12-2, Sat 9-2
Part with £10 of your hard earned cash (£5 on Saturdays) and you'll be given a 'purple dollar' to do with as you wish. Try and resist exchanging it for two pints of lager and a bag of crisps.

Bowling

AMF Bowling
Merrion Centre   245 1781
As this is the only bowling alley left in the city centre it tends to get very busy. If you don't mind being entertained in a windowless basement world, this is the place for you.
£2.80 a game before 6pm, and £3.60 all other times. Shoe hire is £1.

Hollywood Bowl
Cardigan Field Leisure Centre, Kirkstall Road   279 9111
A taste of Hollywood in Kirkstall, except without the stars. Or the glamour. Provides entertainment for families and wayward kids alike. The former have lanes and lanes of bowling to keep them occupied, the latter are able to bunk off and play video games all day. And who says we're a nation of ignoramuses?
£2.50 a game before six, £3.60 after. Shoe hire included.

LA Bowl
Sweet St   242 1330
Slightly out of town but worth the wait if you like to have a choice between bowling and Laser shoot em up games. Adults bowl for £2.50 before 6pm and £3.50 after. Shoe hire is 95p.

TOP FIVE... Play Pool
1. The Elbow Rooms
2. Northern Snooker Ctr
3. Oscars
4. Royal Park Pub
5. Rileys

Galaxy 105   THE NEW MIX FOR YORKSHIRE

...round the main table. Oh I remember ...ose Saturday mornings watching ...diana...

...nooker £3.66 p/h
...ool £4.44 p/h

...iley Snooker Hall
...ross Belgrave Street   243 3391

...he Kwik Save of snooker halls - no frills. ...eople can come to play snooker at any ...me of the day. Only licensed to sell booze ...ormal pub hours though. £10 membership.
...nooker £3.90 p/h
...ool £4.50

Casinos

...rosvenor
...errion Way 244 8386
...oortown Corner 269 5051

...estgate Casino
...irkstall Rd   389 3700

...apoleans Casino
...irkstall Road   2445393

Dance

...orkshire Dance
...t Peter's Buildings
...43 8765

...or those of you who had your own rou-...ne to 'Flashdance' here's the answer to ...our adult dreams (not that kind). It's ...ossible to sign up for just about any kind ...f dance class (not lap dancing, alas) for ...ny age at all levels. I've personally tried ...he 'street dance' class, but no sign of ...eroy unfortunately.

---

great gaming

GROSVENOR CASINOS

starts here

Restaurant & Bars Open 7 Days a Week

2 casinos to choose from

For **FREE** membership call FREEPHONE
08080 21 21 21

Harrogate Rd, Leeds
Merrion Way, Leeds

Open 2pm - 4am daily

Roulette
Blackjack Cardroom
Casino Stud Poker
Punto Banco
Jackpot Machines

Please check individual casinos for gaming facilities

24 hours must elapse between receipt of application and participation in gaming.
Members must be aged 18 years and over.

entertainment

Snooker/Pool Hall

Citrus Pool Bar
North Lane, Headingley   230 2810
New pool hall/bar in Headingley. See Bars section.
Pool £5p/h.

Elbow Room
Call Lane   245 7011
Stacks of tables and a cool environment. Sunday sessions sound fab with an offer on that includes a meal for two with drinks and an hour of pool for fifteen quid. See club section for more details.
£5 per hour during the day, £8 in the evenings

Northern Snooker Centre
Kirkstall Road   243 3015
Nearly 30 full-sized snooker tables alongside 11 American pool tables make this the perfect place to chill if you like your balls potting. No need to worry about booking and getting a game as this joint is open for 21 and a half hours a day. Food is available from the American-style diner so you don't have to leave your break for long. Worth a visit if only to gork at the old school cinema seats

Northern Snooker Centre

9.30am-7am 365 days a year

Stateside AMERICAN CAFE BAR

12noon to midnight 365 days a year

Late bar. Mon-Thur 'til Midnight
Fri & Sat 'til 1am

27 full sized snooker tables
16 American Pool tables
Full bar and food facilities
Satellite and competitions

* **membership offer with card** *

Kirkstall Road, Leeds, LS3 1LT
tel:0113 243 3015
fax:0113 244 3738

THE INDEPENDENT   www.independent.co.uk

The Odeon
The Headrow   0870 5050 007
Slap bang in the middle of town, so a good one to go to if you're planning on drinking afterwards. Licensed bar upstairs open until around 8.30.
Adults £4.70 (£3.30 before 6pm Mon-Fri) NUS £3.30

Showcase
Junction 27 off the M62, Batley   01924 420 622
If it's not on here, it's probably finished. Sixteen-screen monster on the outskirts of Leeds city centre. Late shows mean you can shop 'til you drop at Ikea down the road, then chill out and watch the latest flicks. Ideal. Sort of.
Adults £4.75 (£3.50 before 6pm Mon- Fri) NUS £3.50 £2.50 all day Tuesdays

Warner Brothers
Kirkstall Road   279 9855/ 279 9833
The newest addition to the movie scene in Leeds is about a mile out of town and fairly near to the student areas. Located within a complex with restaurants, leisure centre, nightclub and the like, a whole night out in one visit. Many screens and comfy double seats for you love birds.
Adults £4.70, NUS £3.60.

Theatres

City Varieties
Swan Street   243 0808
Home of the legendary 'Good Old Days' which was filmed live for the BBC from 1953 to 1983, this quaint music hall venue now plays host to stand up comedians, musicals and clairvoyants – but you already knew that, right?

Civic Theatre
Cookridge Street   245 5505
Amateur dramatists dream of staging productions here, as this type of performance is its main staple.

Grand Theatre
New Briggate   222 6222
If you couldn't make it to the big smoke to catch that all important musical, chances are it will tour and visit this grand 1550 capacity venue.

West Yorkshire Playhouse
Quarry Hill Mount   213 7700
One for the less conservative among you as this venue puts on more experimental jaunts in to luvviedom as well as the old favourites. Two theatres of differing capacities housed in one venue. It's also possible to get involved with workshops, lectures and debates which are held regularly. Then you can pop over the road for drinks at The Wardrobe.

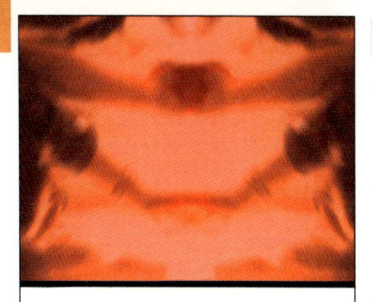

entertainment

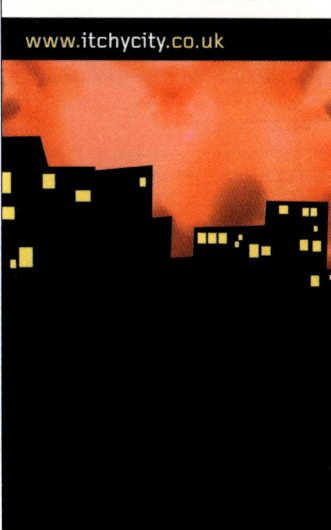

www.itchycity.co.uk

Cinemas

Cottage Road Cinema
Cottage Road, off Otley Road, Headingley   230 2562

Open since 1912, there's none of you fancy multiplex malarkey here. Showin all the main new flicks - but one at a tim in this small but perfectly formed cinema Adults £4.50-£3.50 NUS (Mon/Tues £2.50

Hyde Park Picture House
**Brudenell Road, Hyde Park
275 2045**

As old school as they get, you can actually take your own beer into this beautiful, original Victorian wonder of a cinema Specialises in showing classic flicks Godfather series, Chainsaw Massacre and the like. A cornerstone of the Leed Film Festival held every year. Look ou for special screenings like the Blair Witc one they had last year at midnight, complete with goths.
Adults £3.50 NUS £3.00

Zest

Park Place 234 3133
Pretty cool little sandwich bar with eccentric options and groovy cacti interior. Slimmer Hawaiian baguette £2.45
Mon-Fri; 7am-4pm.

Internet Cafés

Andronicas

Eastgate 246 8844
A cyber-sonic environment in which to surf (consoles upstairs). Remember though that the sexy Californian you're chatting to is probably Bert from Grimsby.
0 mins £1, 30 mins £2.50
Mon-Fri; 8am-7pm, Sat; 10am-6pm

City Cyber

Merrion Centre 242 4008
10 consoles and a one meg lease line make this an attractive place to log on.
15 mins £1.50, 30 mins £2, 1 hour £3.50.
Mon-Fri; 9.30-7.30pm (until 5pm Sat), Sun; 11am-4pm.

Megabyte

Hyde Park Corner 275 4715
Little café in student-central with all the extras and free tea and coffee. Happy hour 10-2 during the week, when students enjoy an hours surfing for £2.50. A lot of them seem to be doing dissertations on porn.
10 mins £1, 30 mins £2.50
Mon-Sat; 10am-8pm, Sun; 12-7pm.

Mouse House

Wellfield Place, Headingley (next to Brett's, behind RSPCA shop) 274 2533
Groovy little place with 7 Mac consoles, and as much tea and coffee as you can drink while you surf.
15 mins £1.50 (£1.20 NUS)
Mon-Fri; 11am-8.30pm, Sat; 11-6.30, Sun; 11-5pm.

City Library

Headrow 247 8282
Three terminals open to the public…and it's free! One hour maximum, and you're advised to book in advance
Mon-Sat; 9.30am-6pm (until 8pm Thurs/ Fri), Sun; 11-5pm.

WH Smith

City Station
A couple of free access terminals.

Sandwich Bars

Bagel Factory
Thorntons Arcade 245 8989
Sit in or take out - choose one of 14 flavours of bagel to house your filling. Also a bagel cart in the city rail station with often very good 99p specials.
Salmon and cream cheese £2.55
Mon-Sat; 8am-5.30pm

French Revolution
Victoria Quarter 234 2290
Excellent take-out only sandwiches, soups and cake that attract big old queues at lunch time.
Club chicken, ham and mayo baguette £2.00
Mon-Sat; 8-5.30pm

Fresse Mucho
Vicar Lane (side of the market) 244 4412
A relaxed atmosphere and excellent freshly made sandwiches that are well worth paying a little more for.
Chicken, bacon and brie tomato melt £3.30
Mon-Fri; 8am-4pm, Sat; 9am-4.30pm

Panninis
St Pauls Rd (off Park Row) 241 6966
Cheery staff and Spanish music in a nice setting to get a speciality pannini to eat in or take out.
Melted ciabatta tuna melt £2.20
Mon-Fri; 7.30-3.30pm

Pret A Manger
Bond Street 234 9423
Well, it's a bit chainy, and the atmosphere is more than a little stiff, but the sandwiches are excellent and it's got nothing to do with France what-so-ever so no frog limbs and the onions are kept to respectable Anglo-Saxon standards.
Veg noodles £2.95
Mon-Sat; 7.30am-5pm, Sun; 11-4pm

Slips Deli
Cardigan Rd, Hyde Park (near the Co-op) 225 0600
Big, tasty subs to take out or eat in accompanied by loud music and bright colours. The best sarnies on a road better known for crack than a snack.
Chicken Saute Sub £3
Mon-Fri; 10.30-10.00pm, Sat/Sun; 10.30-7.30pm

Starbucks
Albion St (245 0511)
Briggate (242 6550)
With probably the most aggressive national expansion since 1939, US coffee culture comes to town with a bang. Despite sheer chaininess, the Briggate branch, with its upstairs room overlooking the busy shopping street, is actually a very attractive place to drink excellent coffee and munch overpriced snacks. Also a branch in the train station.
Brunch Pannini £3.60
Open until 7.30pm Mon/ Tues and Sat, 8pm Wed-Fri and 6.30pm Sun.

Galaxy 105   THE NEW MIX FOR YORKSHIRE

Crusty Bin
The Parade, Headingley 275 2558

It ain't pretty and it ain't big, but this is the standard hangover/post-bender venue for THE fried breakfast that has cured millions of students of the morning after blues. With only four tables, you might have to wait or share, but that breakfast euphoria is worth waiting for. Open from 5am (yes, five) until 4pm everyday.
Breakfast £3

Dare Café
Otley Road, Headingley 230 2828

Now well established as a fine out of town stop off, Dare seems to have rested on its laurels a bit recently. In my opinion, the food, which looks good on paper, is actually pretty average at above average prices. Hopefully it's just a blip in form. Now licensed.
Burritos, £6.50.
Open for breakfast from 9.30am.
Evening restaurant open 'til 10pm.

Café Vitae
Granary Wharf 243 7909

Café chic meets office needs under the arches. Relax, order a coffee and then find yourself that dream job via recruitment web sites or with the help of a qualified consultant. This place is the UK's very first hybrid recruitment consultants and café bar rolled into one – and it's bizarre but pretty impressive.
Mon-Tues, 8am-6pm. Wed-Fri, 8am-8pm. Sat, 9am-6pm. Sun, 11am-5pm.
Tuna fish salad with seasoned butter, lettuce, tomato and cucumber, £5.70.

Grove Café
Brudenell Grove, Hyde Park
230 2727

Take a breather from the city cafes (and their prices) and head on down to studentville. Extensive menu ranging from pizza, burgers and excellent curries. If the music is not to your taste, take your own CDs or chill and listen to the DJs who play once a month.
10% discount with NUS/ UB40. Mon- Fri 4-11, Sat- Sun 11am- 11.30pm

Kada's Coffee Lounge
Crown Street (side of Corn Exchange).

Located just off Assembly Street, this interesting little coffee house is the perfect antidote to the fashionata shenanigans of the rest of the area. Music is provided by local musicians jamming on Saturdays, whilst earlier in the week you can catch some classic movies as you tuck into a mean chicken sandwich.
Mon- Wed 10.30am- Midnight, Thurs- Sat 10.30am-3am, Sun 11.30am- 9.30pm

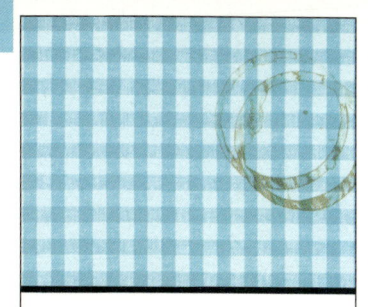

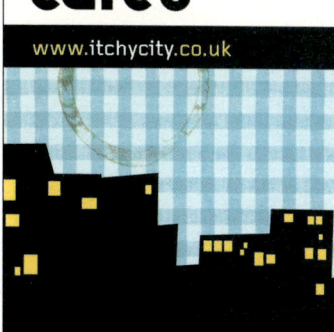

Cafés

Clock Café
Hyde Park Corner 294 5464
Cool eatery, with an alcohol licence an ample seating now provided downstair Serves the best vegetarian breakfast th gal's ever had. A very cool place to wil away a few hours.
Fillet of salmon with sweet chilli ja and new potatoes, £8.45. Serves foo daily from 9.30am-5pm and the 6.30pm-10.30pm.

(Ca) Faluka
Brudenell Road, Hyde Park
The only place outside of the city centr that's open all hours. It's actually sup posed to open 8am-12pm, then 3am 5am but tends to keep its doors ope for as long as there are people chilling Check out the funky keyboard. Foo served right through for those ear morning munchies.

Citrus
North Lane, Headingley (also in th Corn Exchange). 274 9002
Worth the trek into Headingley to enjo a meal or drink in this fab little café Although it's only open until 10pm yo can take your own alcohol. They als own the pool bar next door (see enter tainments), and the café/juice bar in th Corn Exchange (9-5 Mon-Sat, 12-4 Sun serving fresh smoothies and panninis t take away or sit and watch the shopper flit from store to store. Beware th Lemon Mafia – they're taking over.
Panninis £2.50

itchycities...

www.itchycity.co.uk